ELEMENTS OF
SOUTHEASTERN INDIAN RELIGION

INSTITUTE OF RELIGIOUS ICONOGRAPHY
STATE UNIVERSITY GRONINGEN

ICONOGRAPHY OF RELIGIONS

EDITED BY

Th. P. van Baaren, L. P. van den Bosch, L. Leertouwer, F. Leemhuis
H. te Velde, H. Witte, and H. Buning (*Secretary*)

SECTION X: NORTH AMERICA

FASCICLE ONE

LEIDEN
E. J. BRILL
1984

ELEMENTS OF
SOUTHEASTERN INDIAN RELIGION

BY

CHARLES HUDSON

With 48 plates

LEIDEN
E. J. BRILL
1984

ISBN 90 04 06945 3

PRINTED IN THE NETHERLANDS BY E. J. BRILL

In memory of
John J. Honigmann

CONTENTS

BIBLIOGRAPHY

BARTRAM, W., "Observations on the Creek and Cherokee Indians, 1789", *Transactions of the American Ethnological Society*, Vol. III, pt. 1 (1853), pp. 1-81.

CATLIN, G., *Letters and Notes on the Manners, Customs, and Conditions of the North American Indians*, 2 vols., London 1844.

CUSHING, F. H., *A Preliminary Report on the Exploration of Ancient Key-Dweller Remains on the Gulf Coast of Florida*, Proceedings of the American Philosophical Society, vol. XXXV, Philadelphia 1897.

DOCKSTADER, F. J., *Indian Art in America: The Arts and Crafts of the North American Indian*, New York 1973.

DU PRATZ, A. S. L. P., *Histoire de la Louisiane*, Paris 1785.

FUNDABURK, E. L. and M. D. F. FOREMAN, *Sun Circles and Human Hands*, Luverne, Alabama 1957.

GILLILAND, M. S., *The Material Culture of Key Marco, Florida*, Gainesville, Florida 1975.

HARRIOT, T., *A Briefe and True Report of the New Found Land of Virginia*, London 1590.

HOLMES, W. H., "Art in Shell of the Ancient Americans", *Second Annual Report of the Bureau of American Ethnology*, Washington, D.C. 1883.

HUDSON, C., *The Southeastern Indians*, Knoxville, Tennessee 1976.

—— (ed.), *Black Drink: A Native American Tea*, Athens, Georgia 1979.

JEFFRIES, R. W., *The Tunacunnhee Site: Evidence of Hopewell Interaction in Northwest Georgia*, Anthropological Papers of the University of Georgia, No. 1, Athens, Georgia 1976.

KILPATRICK, J. F. and A. G. KILPATRICK, "Eastern Cherokee Folk Tales Reconstructed from the Field Notes of Frans M. Olbrechts", Anthropological Paper no. 80, *Bureau of American Ethnology Bulletin* no. 196, Washington, D.C. 1966.

LORANT, S., *The New World: The First Pictures of America*, New York 1965.

MACCURDY, G. G., "Shell Gorgets from Missouri", *American Anthropologist* 15(1913):395-414.

MILANICH, J. T. and W. C. STURTEVANT (eds.), *Francisco Pareja's 1613 Confessionario: A Documentary Source for Timucuan Ethnography*, Division of Archives, History, and Records Management, Tallahassee, Florida 1972.

MOORE, C. B., "Moundville Revisited", *Journal of the Academy of Natural Sciences of Philadelphia*, Vol. 13, pt. 3 (1907), pp. 337-405.

MORRELL, L. R. and B. C. JONES, "San Juan de Aspalaga (A Preliminary Architectural Study)", *Bureau of Historic Sites and Properties Bulletin* No. 1, Division of Archives, History, and Records Management, Tallahassee, Florida 1970, pp. 25-43.

OLBRECHTS, F. M., *The Swimmer Manuscript: Cherokee Sacred Formulas and Medicinal Prescriptions*, Bureau of American Ethnology Bulletin no. 99, Washington, D.C. 1932.

PENNY, D. W., "The Adena Engraved Tablets: A Study of Art Prehistory", *Midcontinental Journal of Archaeology* 5(1980):10-17.

PHILLIPS, P. and J. A. BROWN, *Pre-Columbian Shell Engravings from the Craig Mound at Spiro, Oklahoman*, paperback edition, part 1, Cambridge, Mass. 1978.

SQUIER, A. M. and E. H. DAVIS, *Ancient Monuments of the Mississippi Valley*, Smithsonian Contributions to Knowledge, vol. 1, Washington, D.C. 1848.

SWANTON, J. R., *Social Organization and Social Usages of the Indians of the Creek Confederacy*, 42nd Annual Report of the Bureau of American Ethnology, Washington, D.C. 1928.

——, *The Indians of the Southeastern United States*, Bureau of American Ethnology Bulletin no. 137, Washington, D.C. 1946.

WARING, A. J. Jr. and P. HOLDER, "A Prehistoric Ceremonial Complex in the Southeastern United States", *American Anthropologist* 47(1945):1-34.

WILLEY, G. R., *An Introduction to American Archaeology*, vol. 1, Englewood Cliffs, N.J. 1966.

WILLOUGHBY, C. C., *The Turner Group of Earthworks, Hamilton County, Ohio*, Papers of the Peabody Museum of American Archaeology and Ethnology, Harvard University, Vol. VIII, No. 3, Cambridge, Mass. 1922.

——, "History and Symbolism of the Muskhogeans", in W. K. Moorehead (ed.), *Etowah Papers*, New Haven, Conn. 1932.

WILSON, A., *American Ornithology*, Philadelphia, c. 1871. Dover reprint, 1975.

INTRODUCTION

The religious beliefs, ritual forms, and modes of artistic expression of the Indians of the southeastern United States are not nearly so well known as those of the Indians who lived in surrounding areas. Many people know about the Iroquois of the northeast with their commemorative wampum belts, their mnemonics made of carved wood, and particularly their disturbingly grotesque masks. The Indians of the Great Lakes region are known for their Midewiwin ceremonialism and their colorful finger-weaving and beadwork. To the West lived the well-known Plains and Prairie Indians, with their nomadic, tipi-dwelling way of life, their dualistic cosmology, Sun Dance ceremony, and geometric art forms. It is ironic that the Southeastern Indians, whose homeland was surrounded by these better known Indians, possessed a cosmology, ritual life, and artistic life that perhaps surpassed all the others, yet for all this the Southeastern Indians are hardly known outside a small circle of specialists.

The Indians of the southeastern United States have rarely appeared in great works of literature or scholarship, and when they have appeared they have been scantily or inaccurately depicted. Chateaubriand—the first French writer who can be called modern—wrote about the Natchez for a large and enthusiastic readership, but Chateaubriand's Indians are Indians in name only. Henry David Thoreau learned about the Green Corn Ceremony of the Southeastern Indians from reading the works of William Bartram (whose reputation as a writer ought to be as widely known as his reputation as a naturalist), and he writes admiringly of this ceremony in *Walden*. William Gilmore Simms had a large readership for his romantic novels and short stories about the Indians of South Carolina, but who today reads Simms or even knows his name? James Frazer mentions the Southeastern Indians in several places in his massive *Golden Bough*. A few stereotypic Indians appear in the short stories of William Faulkner. Beyond this, the religious and symbolic life of the Southeastern Indians has not been the subject of any major works of literature, nor of comparative religion, nor even of anthropology.

THE SOUTHEASTERN CULTURE Area

The Southeastern Culture Area was the region comprising the western bank of the Mississippi River and its hinterland, from about St. Louis southward to the Gulf, and from this area eastward to the southern Atlantic coast and Florida. Above all, the Southeast was an area of large rivers along whose banks rich alluvial soils lay. These rivers included, first and foremost, the lower course of the Mississippi River and its tributaries on both sides, as well as a series of moderately large rivers emptying into the Gulf of Mexico and the Atlantic Ocean. Much of the Southeast consists of flat coastal plain, dotted with slow rivers and swamps. To the north the coastal plain shades off into piedmont and uplands. This zone of transition, where the coastal plain meets the piedmont, was for the Indians a desirable place to live. Many large late prehistoric sites were located in this zone. Mountains intruded into the Southeast in two places: the Appalachian mountains, running down from the northeast, and the Ozark-Ouchita mountains in the west. Because these mountainous areas contained but small amounts of alluvial soils, they never supported large populations of people, but they were good areas for hunting. Moreover, they had the advantage of being cooler in summer, and they were not as mosquito-ridden as the coastal plain and the Gulf and Atlantic Coasts.

The Southeastern Culture Area

Some of the Indian groups who were important in the Southeast in the early eighteenth century were the Upper and Lower Creeks of Alabama and Georgia, the Cherokees of the southern Appalachian mountains, the Chickasaws of northern Mississippi, the Natchez and Choctaws of southern Mississippi, the Caddos of Louisiana and Arkansas, and the Timucua of northern Florida. Smaller groups included the Catawbas of upper South Carolina, the Yuchis, the Calusas of southern Florida, and the Chitimachas of the Lower Mississippi River.

Two natural features favoring horticulture make the Southeast superior to the areas surrounding it. Abundant rainfall sets the Southeast off from the Prairies and Plains, where rainfall declines sharply as one moves west, and its long growing season sets it off from the North, where winters grow progressively longer and colder. But the Southeastern Culture Area cannot be defined solely in terms of natural features. More importantly, in the late Prehistoric period it was an area whose inhabitants resembled each other in the way they conceived of the world.

EARLY PREHISTORY

It is, alas, far more difficult to map the interior world of men's minds than it is to map rainfall or temperature gradients. Some of the broad cognitive patterns which are evident in Southeastern Indian thought may be seen in the belief systems of the Indians of the Northeast, the Great Lakes, the Plains, the Southwest, and even of the Aztecs of the Valley of Mexico. It is reasonable to conclude that some of these similarities are consequences of both the recency and rapidity with which the Americas were populated by people who came from northern Asia. The ancestors of the American Indians arrived in the United States possibly as late as 15,000 years ago. The recency of the human occupation of the New World must be seen in relation to the Old World, where societies of modern and extinct forms of men existed throughout hundreds of thousands of years of time, going all the way back to the origin of our species and our genus. Because of the recency of their coming to the New World, it would not be surprising to find that more fundamental similarities exist among the world views of New World peoples than is the case among Old World peoples.

The earliest Americans, the Paleo-Indians, appear to have made their living by hunting large, late Pleistocene animals. Although they may have possessed a rich symbolism, they did not inscribe, carve, or paint it on durable media, and because of this we know next to nothing about their belief system. Nor is much known about their cultural descendants, the Indians of the Archaic culture, whose way of life prevailed from about 8,000 B.C. until about 1,000 B.C. over a vast portion of North America, stretching from the Rocky Mountains eastward to the Atlantic Coast. The people of the Archaic Culture were similar to each other in making their living by diversified hunting and gathering, but like the Paleo-Indians they bequeathed us next to nothing in term of durable symbolism.

The amount of prehistoric symbolism increased in the eastern United States around 1,000 B.C., when the Woodland cultures began to take shape, particularly along the lower Mississippi River and the drainage of the lower Ohio River. These people evidently continued practicing the Archaic mode of subsistence, though they collected vegetable foods more intensively, and because of this they are thought by some to have possessed the beginnings of horticulture. What changed during the Woodland period is that the Indians began manufacturing elaborate, durable artifacts which were used in ceremonial or artistic contexts, and which therefore serve as evidence of what was symbolically meaningful to them. It is possible, of course, that the minds of the Archaic people were as richly furnished as the minds of their Woodland descendants, but evidence for Archaic ways of thinking is lacking.

In certain places the people of the Archaic culture made and used pottery, but so rarely that when it occurs it is almost a curiosity, and it is so utilitarian that it reveals little, if anything, that can be called symbolic. But during the Woodland period, pottery was manufactured everywhere in the eastern United States, and in its decorations we can first see a symbolism that prefigures that of the Indians we are here calling the Southeastern Indians. In addition, they began making artifacts of carved stone and hammered copper. The most important of these are vessels and artifacts which contain representations of animals, including some of those for which the Southern Indians later had a particular concern: buzzards, falcons, owls, eagles, frogs, serpents, turtles, and cougars, to name a few.

Certain broad elements of design which were important to the Southeastern Indians are first manifested in Woodland artifacts. It should be understood that the conceptions which lay behind these elements of design may have been present in the minds of Archaic Indians, or even Paleo-Indians, but their expression in a durable medium begins with the Woodland people. The design elements include an emphasis on raptorial birds, with curved beaks and talons (Pl. I a. and b.). In some cases beaks, talons, and other features are disarticulated and rearranged.[1] A popular Woodland structural design feature is opposed or split-representations, in which a creature is either split down the middle, so that the two sides, left and right, are then depicted. Or else the intent was to show two different creatures, represented in opposition or conflict. In some cases, the creatures are truly opposed. That is, their overall shapes are the same, but they differ in detail, just as one's left hand resembles one's right, but also differs from it.

At least one Woodland artifact—the Tremper boatstone—represents an important anomalous monster which was frequently depicted in various forms in later Southeastern art. Namely, it is a creature which was generally serpentine in shape, but with horns and sometimes the disarticulated features of other creatures (Pl. II).

Two geometric forms which were important to Woodland Indians (and to later Southeastern Indians) were the circle and the 4-sided (usually square) figure. These show up as motifs incised on stone tablets and ceramics, and also in the form of mounds and earthworks, consisting of low earthen walls, occasionally quite large, and sometimes accompanied by ditches.[2] (Pl. III)

The platform pipe is a characteristic Woodland artifact, so called because the bowl is mounted on a flat, curvate base (Pl. IV). The bowls of these pipes were sometimes plain, but were more commonly fashioned in the form of animals. The presence of these pipes is evidence that like the Indians of later times, the Woodland Indians were smoking one or more substances, and they were probably doing so in a ritual context.[3]

The Woodland Indians resembled later Southeastern Indians in several other respects. For one thing, they fashioned weapons, particularly weights for their spear throwers, with an artistry and care that exceeded mere utility. Whether this was to glorify the role of the warrior (as was later to be the case), or merely the role of the hunter, cannot be known with certainty. Another Woodland practice that was to continue to be practiced by later Southeastern Indians was elaborate burial of the dead. They interred the bodies, bones,

---

[1] David W. Penny, "The Adena Engraved Tablets: A Study of Art Prehistory", *Midcontinental Journal of Archaeology* 5(1980):10-17.

[2] Robert L. Hall, "Ghosts, Water Barriers, Corn, and Sacred Enclosures in the Eastern Woodlands", *American Antiquity* 41(1976):360-364; William Sears, "Food Production and Village Life in Prehistoric Southeastern United States", *Archaeology* 24(1971):322-39.

[3] Robert L. Hall, "An Anthropocentric Perspective for Eastern United States Prehistory", *American Antiquity* 42(1977):499-518.

or cremated remains of certain favored individuals along with grave goods that were often made of materials which originated in far-flung places: mica from the Appalachian Mountains (Pl. V a), copper from the Great Lakes and the Appalachians (Pl. V b), obsidian from the Rocky Mountains, sea shells and shark teeth from the Gulf and Atlantic Coasts. The Woodland Indians also began to build structures of earth. In some cases this earth (and sometimes rocks) was piled up into a mound over the remains of the dead (Pl. VI a). In other cases it was piled up in the form of an animal (Pl. VII), or, as we have already seen, into circles, squares, and other geometrical shapes.

It is difficult to interpret the meaning of Woodland symbolism because it existed at such an early time, and in the Southeast it was superceded by quite a different symbolism, which will be discussed presently. But hints into the meaning of Woodland symbolism and religious practices can be gained from the ethnohistory of Indians who later lived on the margins of the area where the Woodland culture held sway. For example, when the earliest European colonists arrived in North Carolina and Virginia, the Algonkian Indians maintained mortuaries in which the remains of their esteemed dead were kept in a manner reminiscent of the Woodland culture (Pl. VIII); in the late 16th century the Timucuan Indians of the Florida coast still interred their dead beneath small, conical burial mounds (Pl. VI b); and when the Spanish made contact with the 16th century Calusa Indians of southern Florida they retained Woodland-like mortuary practices, still used the spear-thrower as a weapon, and they carved wooden masks (Pl. IX), often in the form of animals, which they wore in ritual contexts.

Beginning around AD 800, in the interior Southeast the Woodland cultures either developed into, or gave way before people bearing a vigorous new economic and social development—the Mississippian culture. Woodland Indians practiced horticulture, but only on a small scale. But the cultivation of corn, beans, and squash was fundamentally important in the Mississippian culture. Populations grew larger, and villages and towns often had strong defensive log palisades built around them. Along with this, a distinctive symbolic system developed and became very widespread. This symbolic system—called the Southern Cult or the Southeastern Ceremonial Complex—will be discussed presently. It was an expression of the culture of the Indians who inhabited the South when the earliest Spanish explorers came in the 16th century.

Unfortunately, these earliest explorers were little interested in this symbolic system, so that the accounts of their travels are of little help in explicating the meaning of the symbols. Moreover, in their wake they brought in epidemic diseases which caused such a collapse of population, and therefore of societies, that many of the symbols appear to have no longer been employed when the next European observers penetrated the interior of the Southeast a little over a century later.

This breakdown in the belief system of the Southeastern Indians and its attendant symbolism was made even more complete in the early 19th century, when most of the Indians were "removed" from the Southeast. That is, as impediments to a rapidly expanding and profitable plantation agriculture, they were forced to abandon their homeland and move west of the Mississippi River. Only a handful of Cherokees, Choctaws, Seminoles, Catawbas, and Creeks managed, by one means or another, to evade removal and remain in the Southeast.

Hence the documentation of the symbolic and religious life of the Southeastern Indians is extraordinarily uneven. During the Mississippian period the Indians possessed a rich symbolic system, a sample of which was fortunately preserved on shell and pottery, and they must have possessed and elaborate belief system and religious life to go along with it, but no texts are available from this period to explicate the symbols. Texts are available from the late 19th century and early 20th century, particularly for the Cherokees, but their symbolism and religious life by this time were greatly eroded.

LATE PREHISTORY:
THE SOUTHEASTERN CEREMONIAL COMPLEX

At about 800 AD a fundamental economic and social transformation occurred among the Indians of the late prehistoric Southeast. This transformation drastically changed the culture of the Southeastern Indians, and it generated a new and different symbolic system. Occurring in most parts of the Southeastern area, as previously defined, and not much outside it, the archaeological manifestation of this transformation is known as the Mississippian culture.

When the symbolic system that accompanied it was first identified by Antonio Waring and Preston Holder in the late 1930s and early '40s, it was called the "Southern Cult".[4] More recently it is called the "Southeastern Ceremonial Complex."[5] It was defined on the basis of a series of artifacts found at the Etowah mounds in Georgia, the Moundville site in Alabama, and the mounds near Spiro, Oklahoma, and to a lesser extent from materials found at the Citico Mound and the Castalian Springs site in Tennessee, as well as at Mount Royal and Key Marco in Florida, and elsewhere. As described by Waring and Holder, the Southeastern Ceremonial Complex was manifested in a series of motifs, representations of deities (or people impersonating deities), weapons, and certain items of costume which occurred in all or most of these sites.

These motifs include the equal-armed or Greek Cross; circles, often with scalloped edges, or with crosses contained within them; the "bilobed arrow", an enigmatic motif consisting of an arrow with crescent-shaped lobes on either side; the forked-eye design; the barred oval; open hands with eyes or other small motifs depicted in the palms; and skulls and limb bones (Pl X). The representations of deities or spirits (or perhaps costumed dancers) include, principally, the falcon, or a man dressed as a falcon; the crested woodpecker; the "rattlesnake", sometimes depicted with horns and other anomalous features; and cougars, some of whom possess some decidedly unfeline characteristics (Pl. XI; XIII; XIV).

The ceremonial objects (Pl. XII) which were important in the Southeastern Ceremonial Complex include gorgets made of shell and copper; pendants made from conch shell columnellas; sheets of embossed copper; hair ornaments in the form of bilobed arrows, plumes, or war clubs; ear spools which were worn through slits made along the lower margins of the ears; various kinds of celts and war-clubs; pipes for smoking

---

[4] Antonio Waring and Preston Holder, "A Prehistoric Ceremonial Complex in the Southeastern United States", *American Anthropologist* 7(1945):1-34.
[5] James H. Howard, *The Southeastern Ceremonial Complex and its Interpretation*, Missouri Archaeological Society Memoir No. 6, 1968.

tobacco and other substances; conchshell drinking cups; fancy ceramic bottles; and discoidal gaming stones. Items of costume include hair knots worn at the back of the head; ear spools; the hair ornaments already mentioned; a long forelock worn dangling over the forehead with beads strung on it; beaded bands worn about the arms and legs; sashes tied about the waist, often with the ends hanging down; and an enigmatic pointed pouch or apron worn suspended from the waist. Personages in the iconography are shown brandishing war clubs, knives, bows and arrows, and in some cases human heads.

It has been far easier to define the Southeastern Ceremonial Complex than it has been to discover its meaning. One early theory was that the Complex represented a nativistic cult which spread rapidly in the wake of the De Soto expedition of 1539-43 and the epidemic diseases which followed it. It was thought to have been similar to the Ghost Dance of the western United States in the nineteenth century. Because some of the motifs are reminiscent of motifs in late prehistoric Mexico, it was even proposed that the Southeastern Ceremonial Complex was the result of proselytization on the part of Mexican Indian servants who were brought into the Southeast by Tristan de Luna in his expedition of 1559-61,[6]

To others, however, it was clear that the Southeastern Ceremonial Complex represented a phenomenon whose roots went back much further than 1539.[7] And the archaeological research that has been done in the past 30 years or so has bourne this out. What this research has shown is that beginning around AD 800 the Southeastern Indians began practicing maize agriculture. They had been cultivating squash for a long time, beginning even before the Woodland period. But squash is easy to cultivate. It is so easy to cultivate that it requires no re-scheduling of activities, no re-arrangement of priorities, no revaluation of land. Maize, on the other hand, requires people to labor and to plan their activities to suit its growing cycle (Pl. XV a). Maize has to be tended, and it has to be protected from insects and predators. Moreover, it requires plentiful nutrients, particularly nitrogen, and if fertilizer is not used (and the Indians used none) the land on which the maize is to be cultivated has to be rich. This is why the Southeastern Indians placed such a premium on the rich alluvial soils that occur along the rivers and creeks of the Southeast.

The commitment of the Southeastern Indians to a horticultural way of life was even plainer around AD 1000, when beans appear to have first been cultivated. When maize is complemented by beans, the two constitute a relatively complete vegetable diet. With these two cultigens the Mississippian people became capable of supporting a relatively dense population with a horticultural economy. However, even though the people of the Mississippian period may have been able to subsist by horticulture alone, the hunting and gathering of wild foods still remained important in their diet, and it remained so well into the historic period (Pl XV b).

Along with this heightened dependence on horticulture—and with it, no doubt, a reorganization of their habits of life and their world view—their population increased. Whether this increase in population stimulated their dependence on horticulture, or

---

[6] James B. Griffin, "The De Luna Expedition and the 'Buzzard Cult' in the Southeast", *Washington Academy of Sciences Journal* 34(1944):299-303.
[7] Antonio J. Waring, Jr., "The De Luna Expedition and the Southeastern Ceremonial", *American Antiquity* 11(1945):57-58.

whether it was the other way around, may be debated. But whichever was the case, villages and towns grew larger, ceremonial and ritual life became more elaborate, and also there is indirect evidence for the existence of larger and more complicated political entities. This is particularly evident in their building quite large earthern mounds in certain places which served as the foundations on which they built temples and other structures (Pl. XVI; XVII a and b).

It is also clear that along with these economic and social changes, in some places and at some times the level of warfare increased. This is plainly evident in some of the towns which were surrounded by substantial log palisades, often with strong log towers on which defenders could stand and shoot arrows and hurl other weapons downward at attackers (Pl. XVIII a and b).

This economic and social transformation which led to greater dependence on horticulture and to a more complex social order is one of the keys to understanding the nature and meaning of the Southeastern Ceremonial Complex. But by itself this transformation is not sufficient to explain it, because the Southeastern Ceremonial Complex was a mixture of old and new. Moreover, it was no simple list of old and new elements; rather it was a complex of structural patterns, some of which were old, and therefore widespread in the New World, plus new elements, some of which were unique to the Southeast.

The circle and the square (including the Greek cross) must represent conceptions that are exceedingly old in the New World. We have already seen that they were present in the iconography of the Woodland Period in the eastern United States, and their occurrence in many other parts of the New World must mean that they represent conceptions much older than the Woodland period. Both of these structural patterns survived into historic times in the Southeast, and some insight into their meaning can be gained from myths and rituals dating from this period. For example, many Southeastern dances called for circular movements and formations, and the winter council house was laid out with a circular floor plan. In contrast, the summer council house had a square ground plan, with four open cabins facing in upon a small courtyard. Both were related to the fundamental way in which the Indians conceived of the cosmos and particularly the antithetical or opposed forces which bore in upon a "center" (Pl. XIX-XX).

Perhaps the single most important theme in the Southeastern Ceremonial Complex is warfare[8], and this, as we have seen, appears to have been a concomitant of the increased dependence upon horticulture and therefore of the preminum that came to be placed on rich riverine soils. It was a hand-to-hand, terroristic kind of warfare, fought with the bow and arrow, but more particularly with the war club (Pl. XXI).

Hence, some of the most striking Southeastern Ceremonial Complex works depict warriors running along brandishing knives, clubs, maces, and war-axes, and sometimes holding the severed heads of their victims by the hair. Other warlike motifs include arrow points, arrows, and scalplocks. The flavor of this kind of warfare is best indicated in those instances where the war clubs ("maces") are shown as being broken, and sometimes forearm bones are shown broken as well.[9] (Pl. XXII-XXIII).

---

[8] James A. Brown, "The Southern Cult Re-Considered", *Midcontinental Journal of Archaeology* 1976(1):125-128.

[9] Philip Phillips and James A. Brown, *Pre-Columbian Shell Engravings from the Craig Mound at Spiro, Oklahoma*, paperback edition, volume I (Cambridge: Peabody Museum Press, 1978), plates 55, 56, 57, 58.

In a few instances people are depicted as being killed (and perhaps tortured) while having their hands and feet tied to rectangular frames (Pl. XXIV a and b). They are shown being shot with arrows, and in at least one instance decapitated heads are shown.[10] It cannot be known with certainty whether this represents the torture and killing of war prisoners, as practiced by the Natchez in the early eighteenth century, or sacrifice similar to the Morning Star sacrifice of the Skidi Pawnee, or some other completely unknown Mississippian ritual.

A second theme that is evident in the Southeastern Ceremonial Complex is that differences in social status existed and were important. This is most clearly seen in the mortuary practices (Pl. XXV a and b). Some individuals were buried with far more pomp and circumstance than others. This is shown by their being interred in or near the big mounds and ceremonial centers. In some instances they were carried to the burial site on litters made of cedar poles, bourne on the shoulders of their people, and heaped with conch shells, pottery bottles, pipes, axes, war clubs, ear spools, beads, and copper plates.[11] In some cases, retainers were killed and buried with them. Some of these honored individuals were clearly warriors, while others were probably political leaders and priests.

During the Mississippian period the Southeastern Indians are thought to have been organized into chiefdoms, a form of political organization midway in complexity between an egalitarian tribal organization and a centralized state governed by an hereditary elite. Chiefdoms may be small or large, and they may be more or less centralized. In smaller, less centralized chiefdoms, status is generally acquired through merit, but in the more centralized chiefdoms status may be acquired by birth alone. Unfortunately, it is by no means an easy task to distinguish between ascribed and achieved status solely on the basis of archaeological evidence. But it is safe to say that some of the honored individuals in Mississippian burials were members of powerful chiefly lineages.

A third theme in the Southeastern Ceremonial Complex is the game of chunkey, a variant of the hoop and pole game which was played by Indians throughout North America (Pl. XXVI, a-c). Chunkey was distinctive, however, in that it was played with a disc made of finely polished stone instead of a wooden hoop. The Mandans of the Missouri River also played the game with a stone disc. Two men at a time competed against each other in the game. One rolled the chunkey stone along the ground while both players cast poles in the direction the disc was rolling. Points were scored depending upon how close the players' poles came to the disc when it stopped rolling and fell over. They competed fiercely and bet heavily on the outcome.

A second game, stickball—a form of lacrosse—was also important to the Southeastern Indians. It was played by large teams, sometimes with hundreds of players, and the teams typically came from different towns. The players carried pairs of ballsticks, or raquets, each about the length of the warclubs of which they were so fond. The object of the game was to score a certain number of points by throwing or carrying a small ball across a goal. They were not permitted to touch the ball with their hands. Because it was a rough game, in which the players used much the same skills they used in hand-to-hand combat in war-

---

[10] Ibid., pp. 108, 109, 181.
[11] Phillips and Brown, p. 13. Henry W. Hamilton, Jean Tyree Hamilton, and Eleanor F. Chapman, *Spiro Mound Copper*, Missouri Archaeological Society Memoir, no. 11 (1974).

fare, it was called "the little brother of war." For reasons that are not entirely clear, the game of stickball was seldom if ever depicted in Southeastern Ceremonial Complex art, but after European colonization and domination, chunkey ceased to be played, while stickball remained popular throughout the nineteenth century, and to some extent it is still played today.

A fourth major theme or characteristic of the Southeastern Ceremonial Complex is that it is full of animal symbolism. That this profusion of animals incised on shell or embossed on copper represents no mere love of animals may be seen in the fact certain animals and parts of animals are depicted far more frequently than others. Like the people of the Woodland period, Mississippian people were fond of birds, and particularly falcons (Pl. XXVII a). Many of these falcons were embossed on sheets of copper. In some cases what is depicted is a naturalistic rendering of the bird itself; or the body of a falcon is shown with a human head. In other cases it is obviously a human dressed as a falcon, with a tail, a cape representing wings, and wearing a mask. In still other cases a warrior is represented with the forked-eye marking of a falcon. It is also likely that the pointed pouch or apron, which resembles the downy feathers between and below a falcon's legs, was meant to make the wearer resemble this bird (Pl. XXVII b).

Like the falcon, many of the other animals depicted in the Southeastern Ceremonial Complex are aggressive. This includes the rattlesnake, the cougar, and the spider (Pl. XXVIII a and b). Others are the turkey gobbler, which can be remarkably aggressive in certain seasons, and whose long dangling, black breast feathers reminded the Indians of a human scalplock (Pl. XXIX a and b), and the woodpecker, a bold aggressive bird whose behavior evidently reminded them of their fighting with warclubs (Pl. XXX a and b). In some places the raccoon is important, though for reasons that are not well understood. Often these raccoons are shown wearing beaded bands about their wrists, ankles, and waists (Pl. XXXI a).

The most interesting, and also the most enigmatic subject in the Southeastern Ceremonial Complex is the anomalous creatures which combine the features of several different animals. These often have the body of a rattlesnake, but also the horns of a deer, the head of a cougar, or the wings and sometimes the talons of a bird.[12] In other cases the body of the creature is basically that of a cougar, and to this the features of other animals are added (Pl. XXXI b).

Beyond these anomalous creatures, whose parts are at least those of identifiable creatures, there are a few examples of even more fantastic animals and conceptions. They no doubt represent concepts or images which may have been immediately and fully intelligible to the Mississippian Indians, but which are at present unintelligible to us. Several of these strange creatures have been found on the shell engravings from the Spiro site (Pl. XXXII-XXXIII).

These creatures of the imagination are the ones which are the most difficult to interpret. But as we shall presently see, enough mythological material was collected from the Cherokees in the nineteenth and twentieth centuries to provide us with some insight into these murkier parts of the Southeastern Ceremonial Complex.

One of the puzzling omissions in the Southeastern Ceremonial Complex is that relatively little of the iconography deals explicitly with agriculture, and agriculture, as we

---

[12] Phillips and Brown, Ibid., pp. 141-143.

have seen, is thought to have been the stuff which gave the Mississippian culture its momentum. One possible exception is a small number of shell engravings which depict men performing rituals, and some of these possibly had some connection with agricultural ceremonialism similar to the Green Corn Ceremony, to be discussed later (Pl. XXXIV a and b).

THE CHEROKEE COSMOS

The first sustained ethnographic field work conducted in the Southeast was done among the eastern Cherokees from 1887 to 1890 by James Mooney, an anthropologist who worked for the Bureau of American Ethnology. Subsequently anthropologists such as John R. Swanton and Frank Speck did field research on other Southeastern Indians, both in the Southeast and in Oklahoma. But none of this later work reveals as much about the inner world of the Southeastern Indians as Mooney's research. A close reading of the myths, sacred formulas, and ritual practices collected by Mooney shows that even in the late nineteenth century his Cherokee informants still possessed a reasonably coherent world view, though one which was no doubt but a remnant of what it formerly had been. Mooney's success was largely his because he won the trust and cooperation of Swimmer, a monolingual Cherokee medicineman and keeper of traditions (Pl. XXXV a). Mooney discovered that Swimmer and other Cherokee medicine men kept little books in which they wrote down their sacred knowledge using the syllabary invented by Sequoyah in the early nineteenth century, and in so doing they had produced a nacent sacred literature (Pl. XXXV b).

Some of the more important structural features of the Cherokee belief system can be summarized in the form of a series of propositions about the nature of the cosmos. To some degree these Cherokee propositions hold for the belief systems of other Southeastern Indians, though the full extent to which they were pan-Southeastern can never be known because no other Southeastern mythologies are comparably rich. Moreover, it is clear that this Cherokee belief system sheds light on the meaning of certain aspects of the Southeastern Ceremonial Complex and of Mississippian iconography.[13]

1. *Mythical time preceded world time and was different from it.* The Cherokees believed that the order of the world in which they lived was created in mythical time. It was during this time of chaos that mud was raised from beneath the waters, whereupon it spread out and grew to form the island earth. It was in mythical time that all beings, including archetypical man and woman, came to earth (Pl. XXXVI). And it was in mythical time that the clever water spider skipped across the surface of the water to an island where Thunder, a great spirit, had placed fire. The water spider brought back a live coal in a basket which she carried on her back, and thus it was that men acquired fire. It was in world time that ordinary people lived.

2. *The Cosmos has three levels: this world (the earth), the upper world, and the under world.* Initially, all was water, with the sky above enclosed by a vault, which they believed was made of a hard substance, like rock. The island earth, as already mentioned, was created when mud was brought up from beneath the waters. Many spiritual beings were believed

[13] C. Hudson, *The Southeastern Indians* (Knoxville, Tenn.: University of Tennessee Press, 1976), pp. 120-183.

to live above the vault of the sky, including large versions of all the animals which existed on earth. The under world existed beneath the earth and the waters. Streams of water were pathways to the under world, and the springs at their heads were doorways through which one could enter the under world. The under world was populated by spirits and monstrous beings. The under world was chaotic: there the normal things and conditions of this world were turned upside down. The seasons in the under world were the opposite of seasons on earth. One can prove this by immersing one's hand in a spring of water: in winter the water feels warmer than the outside air, but in summer it feels cooler.

3. *The Cherokees live at the center of the world, and from here there are four cardinal directions, each with different values.* The red east was the direction of vitality, life, and conflict; its opposite, the black west, was the direction of dissolution, death, and decay. The white south was the way of harmony, wisdom, and social solidarity; its opposite, the blue north, was the direction of divisiveness, social disorder, and witchcraft. Many Cherokee rituals required that ritual actions, such as blowing puffs of tobacco smoke, be done in each of the four cardinal directions. The circle and cross motif of the Southeastern Ceremonial Complex probably symbolized this conception.

4. *The principle of vengeance is such that when a being of one category injures a being of another category, the members of the category sustaining the injury seek vegeance.* This principle was remarkably pervasive in Cherokee thought. They assumed that it governed relationships between creatures as well as between creatures and spirits. In the realm of human society, the principle of vengeance was the basis of the most important Cherokee legal principle—*lex talionis*: an eye for an eye, a tooth for a tooth. As well, the Cherokees believed that people could cause injury to animals by killing them improperly, and when this happened the animals could seek vengenace for the injury.

5. *The microcosm resembles the macrocosm.* Man and society were the models by which the earth and the cosmos were conceived. Man was the model of the earth. For example, human blood was to fire as saliva was to water in streams. Since water and fire were believed to be opposites, water was not to be poured upon a fire, and likewise, one was not supposed to spit into a fire. On the other hand, it was quite all right to put blood or meat into a fire. In fact, a successful hunter customarily threw a small piece (usually a piece of liver) of a butchered game animal into fire as an offering.

In accordance with this same microcosm-macrocosm principle, a good person was supposed to seek to maintain harmony in society as well as harmony in his relationships with the spirit world. And if disharmony occurred either in human society or in the spirit world, illness and trouble were likely to occur.

6. *All things possess spirit; some spirits exist in their own right; and all spirits exist in a special mode of existence.* Ordinarily, spirits could not be seen, though certain individuals were believed to have the power to see them. All spirits possessed certain human emotions, as, for example, when injured they became angry and sought vengeance. In mythical time all spirits could communicate with each other, so that people, animals, and plants could communicate easily with each other. But in world time, the time of existing people, the spirits of different kinds of beings could communicate with each other only under special circumstances.

Spirits were believed to be neither intrinsically good nor intrinsically evil. Rather, they were harmful or helpful depending upon circumstances. Since the same kind of rivalries were believed to exist among spirits as existed among living beings, when curing a patient a medicine man would often adopt the strategy of artfully setting one spirit against another.

The most important Cherokee spirit was the Sun, who was thought to be an old woman. They called her "grandparent". She was the source of all warmth and light. Sacred fire was her representative on earth, and for this reason men were supposed to do nothing profane in the presence of sacred fire. The Cherokees addressed prayers only to the Sun (and to sacred fire); they attempted to command or manipulate lesser spirits in a more direct fashion.

Other Cherokee spirits were the Moon, who was believed to be the Sun's brother and who was thought to have some control over rain and snow; the River, also called "Long Man" or "Long Snake", which was a vehicle of purification, such that one of the most important Cherokee rituals of purification was performed at the edge of the river; and Thunder, the Red Man of the east, who was a friend of the Cherokees, and whose two sons, the Two Little Red Men, were often called upon in times of need. In addition, a full complement of animal spirits existed at the four corners of the cosmos: a red otter, falcon, bear, etc., to the east; a white complement of the same to the south; a black complement to the west; and a blue complement to the north.

7. *All the beings of the world are divided into categories, some of which are closer to the realm of spirit than others.* Beings included animals, plants, and people. Among the animals, owls and cougars were believed to have been special because they had the ability to see at night, and hence they had a hunter's advantage over all diurnal animals. Among plants, ceder, pine, spruce, holly, and laurel were special because all of them kept their green foliage the year around, thus seeming to remain young forever. Among people it was those individuals who were priests, medicine men, and sorcerers who were able to fast and to deal with spirits. The most powerful men were called *ada· we· hi*—men who possessed the highest spiritual ability.

Each of the great categories of beings was further subdivided into smaller categories, and each category was distinct. In the realm of people, males differed from females. Their natures were believed to have been radically different, and they could be dangerous to each other, as for example, a menstruating woman was believed to be so dangerous she was required to go into seclusion for several days.

In the realm of animals, the main subcategories were the four-footed animals—the creatures of the surface of the earth; birds, creatures of the air, and hence the animals who were closest to the realm of spirit; and vermin, including snakes and fish, creatures of the watery under world (Pl. XXXVII a).

Each of the four-footed animals had its own personality and character. Principal among the four-footed animals was the Virginia deer, no doubt because the deer was the main game animal for the Cherokees. The dog was an animal which was believed to be peculiarly close to man; so close, in fact, that the medicine which was believed to make a man into a witch could be administered to a dog, which thereafter became an infallible tracker of game (Pl. XXXVII b). As a final example, the rabbit was believed to be a trickster and a mischief maker.

Each bird had a distinct character, and the world of birds was a metaphorical mirror of the world of men. The bald eagle, supreme chief of the birds, with its white head, was the majestic bird which soared serenely above all the contention and wrangling which occurred below (Pl. XXXVII c). The fierce, combative falcon was the bird which was beloved by young warriors. In particular, the peregrine falcon was the one which could dart swiftly down from a height and kill another bird on the wing. The crow was a thief and a raucous detractor who often ganged up to harass hawks and falcons. The horned owl, with its mysterious nocturnal habits and its weird cry, was a witch among birds (Pl. XXXVIII a and b). Its ability to see in darkness gave it an unfair advantage over other birds, and the Cherokees had a single word *tshki·li*, which meant both "horned owl" and "witch". The cardinal, with its beautiful red plumage, was said to have been the daugther of the Sun. Even the smallest birds had their own special characteristics. The tiny Carolina chickadee was believed to be a truthteller, and to hear one while on the trail gladdened the heart of a traveler far away from home. But the tufted titmouse, whose song closely resembles that of the Carolina chickadee, was a liar. Hence, the traveler had to ask himself, "Which bird was that? Chickadee or titmouse?" Just as one has to separate truth from falsehood when dealing with people.

Among the vermin, the principal species were the rattlesnake, the copperhead, and the spreading adder. In Cherokee mythology, all of these snakes were believed to have originally been men who had been transformed into serpents by the Two Little Red Men. One of the three, the rattlesnake, was clearly paramount. The Cherokees addressed the rattlesnake as "grandparent", the same term they used when addressing the Sun. They refrained from killing rattlesnakes because they feared that they would be bitten by a snake in retaliation, in accordance with the principle of vengeance.

8. *Beings which conform to more than one major category are anomalous and are treated or regarded in a special way.* Anomalous creatures were those which did not fit neatly into a single category, but which fell into two or more. Such creatures, as we have already seen, were frequently represented in the art of the Southeastern Indians during the Mississippian period.

The creature which overlapped the animal and human categories was the bear. The bear was an animal, but its habit of sometimes walking bipedally and of eating the same kinds of foods as people gave it a human quality. In many Cherokee myths, the bear is depicted as a big, clumsy fool, who thinks well of himself because of his size and great strength, but who constantly loses out to smaller but sharper-witted creatures (Pl. XXXIX a).

The Venus fly trap and the pitcher plant overlapped the plant and animal categories. Both are plants, but both "catch" insects and "eat" them. The roots of both of these plants were important in medical and ritual contexts.

Each of the three main categories of animals had one or more anomalies at their intersections with each other. The flying squirrel and the bat overlapped the bird and four-footed categories; the frog, turtle, and otter overlapped the four-footed and vermin categories, since all of these were animals which were at home both on land and in water; and the kingfisher overlapped the bird and vermin categories because it is a bird, but builds its nest in a small burrow in a bank of earth, and it dives into the water to catch small fish (Pl. XXXIX b and c).

But by far the most anomalous being in the Cherokee world view was the *uktena*, a creature which was believed to have the body of a rattlesnake, though it was much larger, and to have the horns of a deer on its head, and wings upon its back. Moreover, it partook of the human, since it was believed to have originally been a human who was transformed into its dreadful shape by the Two Little Red Men. On its forehead the uktena had a crystal which gave off blazing flashes of light. It was called the *u·lahsathi* crystal, and anyone who owned one could look into it and divine the future (see below). It is quite clear that the Cherokee regarded the *uktena* as a being, not a spirit. And clearly, the *uktena* was similar to the serpentine monsters depicted in the Southeastern Ceremonial Complex.

CHEROKEE CURING

The ritual life of the Cherokees was logically and symbolically consistent with their belief system, and this included their concepts of disease and of how disease could be cured. In particular, they believed that many diseases were caused by disturbances in their world, whether in their social relationships or in their relation with the cosmos. A disturbance, imbalance, or rupture of good order could only be set right through ritual means.

For example, the Cherokees believed that a person could have his "saliva spoiled" by the evil-intentioned actions of another person in his community. In accordance with the microcosm-macrocosm principle, saliva was to the individual as water in creeks and rivers was to the world. It was a vital element through which pollution was expelled, and if one's saliva were spoiled, it was a serious matter.

One's saliva could be spoiled either by a sorcerer (a "man-killer") or a witch (a *tshki·li*: a nefarious night-goer). The actual mechanism by which one's saliva was spoiled was mysterious, but the identity of the agent who caused the condition could be discovered, though the procedures might be expensive and difficult. A sorcerer worked his magic for intelligible reasons and by known means, though the victim might have to consult with a medicine man to discover what these reasons and means were. What usually lay behind an instance of sorcery was a slight or an injury, real or imagined, to another person. Hence in a case of sorcery, the disturbed relationship was a consequence of a person's own doing.

To have one's saliva spoiled by a witch was far more serious because a witch was intrinsically evil and therefore existed outside the pale of humanity. A witch attacked his or her victim not in retaliation for a slight or an injury, but simply because the victim was vulnerable. In many cases, the witch attacked a victim who was already ill, a woman in childbirth, or young, sickly children.

The symptoms of spoiled saliva were dejection and despondency, what we today call depression. Another symptom of this illness was dreaming of snakes or fish, both of which are inhabitants of the watery under world.

Although uncertainty surrounded a witch's identity and a witch's actions, the Cherokees had a clear conception of how one became a witch. One had merely to fast and drink an infusion of a peculiar root which resembled a beetle with the stem of the plant growing out of its mouth (perhaps *Sagittaria latifolia*, Willd.). In spring and early summer, when it was dark the stem of this plant was said to give off a purplish glow, the color of witchcraft. If a person fasted for four days and drank this decoction it enabled him to transform himself into any creature living on the surface of the earth—a dog, deer, any person, etc. If a person fasted for seven days and drank it, he was additionally able to transform himself into a creature of the air—an owl, a raven—and into a creature that traveled beneath the earth, e.g. a mole. A witch of the seventh degree was also believed to travel about at night in the form of a spark of purple light, moving noiselessly through the air.

Because sick people and women in labor were vulnerable to witches, the relatives and friends of such people would come to their homes and remain awake at night to protect them. As a means of divining the activities of witches, they would heap up a small mound of coals and ashes to one side of a hearth, perhaps as a symbolic representation of this world or of the cosmos. Occasionally they would sprinkle fine particles of sacred tobacco (*Nicotiana rustica*) onto the mound. When a particle burst into flame, it indicated the direction from which a witch was approaching. If it burst into flame in the center of the mound, it meant that the witch was directly overhead. If it burst into flame with a pop, it meant that the witch was about to enter the cabin. The Cherokees believed that a witch could be killed by simply discovering and revealing his or her identity.

Just as illness could be caused by a disturbance in one's social relations, an illness could also be caused by a disturbance in the cosmos. Diseases existed in the realm of spirit, hence they could enter the body invisibly and unnoticed. The Cherokee word for disease (*uyugi*) carried the sense of "resentment", implying that disease was caused by a real or fancied injury to some creature or being. Such diseases entered the body in a mysterious way, and once there, they could lay dormant for months or even years before they manifested themselves.

In most cases, illness caused by a disturbance in the cosmos was set in motion by the breaking of a ritual rule or avoidance. The entire belief system of the Cherokees was embroidered by an intricate series of such rules. For example, people were supposed to treat animals respectfully so as not to incur their anger. Upon killing a deer, a hunter was supposed to beg forgiveness for having taken its life. And the offal of the butchered animal was not to be strewn about for dogs to eat, but rather it was to be burned in a fire. Moreover, both fire and the river were to be treated with respect. One should not, for example, spit into a fire, nor urinate into a river. It made no difference whether such rules were broken on purpose or inadvertently. The consequences were the same.

When a person realized that he was ill, he consulted with a medicine man. Since the cause of a disease cou[...] [...]ears in the past, and since a disease could [...] [...] would question his patient closely about l[...] [...]es and neighbors. He also questioned his p[...] [...]ms that he had had. Again, such dreams [...] [...]ree years.

Depending upon h[...] [...] medicine man then decided upon applyin[...] [...] from a swelling, the medicine man might [...] [...]e live coals or a fire and then massage the[...]

If the patient suffer[...] [...] medicine man might decide to scratch him[...] [...]ration was generally done with an arrowhe[...] [...]berry briar might be used, and in the past rattlesnake fangs were used. The loss of blood through scratching was thought to enhance the suppleness of joints. It was for this reason that Cherokee athletes were ceremonially scratched many times by means of a comb-like instrument (*kanuga*) before a game of stickball (Pl. XLI a).

When the cause of a disease was determined to have become intruded into the patient's body, a sucking horn made from a segment of animal horn was applied to the affected part. The medicine man applied it to the affected part by sucking some air from beneath it with his lips, creating a vacuum. When the horn eventually fell off the patient's body, the medicine man then looked inside it for an object. He sometimes found a small pebble, worm, or insect in the horn, no doubt put there by sleight of hand.

In addition to mechanical means of curing, the Cherokees also made use of an extensive series of herbal medicines (Pl. XLI b). These were made from the leaves, bark, and roots of various plants, some of which were undoubtedly efficacious. Others were chosen on homeopathic grounds. For example, to cure a patient who was obsessed by the memory of a dead relative, the medicine man might prepare a decoction from the thimbleberry shrub which grew high up in the cavity of a hollow tree. Like the manner in which the medicine man tore away the shrub's roots, which clung stubbornly to the tree, so the memory of the dead person would be pulled out of the mind of his patient.[14]

These herbs were generally collected fresh, just before they were administered. They were then powdered and placed in cold or boiling water, whichever was deemed appropriate. Then the patient either drank the medicine, sometimes in surprisingly large quantities, or else the medicine man used a tube to blow the medicine in a spray onto the patient's body.

Correct words were as important in a cure as correct medicines. Here, for example, is a formula that was uttered by the medicine man for a patient who dreamed of being bitten by a snake. Such a dream, or nightmare, was treated as if the snake bite had been actual.

> Ya! Ha! now, Black Snake, they have caused thee to come down it seems. The Snake (that has bitten him) is only a ghost, it seems. They have caused thee to come down, it seems.
>
> The ever-living bones, the ever-living teeth it has advanced toward him, it seems. It was only a black snake that laid itself about the trail, it seems. But right now, it feigned to bite thee, it seems. Ha! now thou hast become faltering.
>
> But now the ever-living bones have been made weak; thou are now in such a condition. There has been hesitation (on thy part) it seems. Ha! now thou hast become faltering.
>
> But at this very moment you Two Little Men, you Two Powerful Wizards, they have caused you to come down. It was a black snake, it seems, but the snake is merely a ghost (and) it has feigned to put the disease under him, it seems; (it thought) its track would never be found. But now you have come to take it away. Where the black boxes are, you two have gone to store it up. As soon as you two have turned round, relief will have been caused at the same time.[15]

---

[14] James Mooney, *The Swimmer Manuscript: Cherokee Sacred Formulas and Medical Prescriptions*, Bureau of American Ethnology Bulletin 99 (Washington, D.C., 1932), p. 53.

[15] James Mooney, *The Swimmer Manuscript*, p. 176.

The medicine man hoped that his patient's saliva had been spoiled by a snake that he had offended. Hence, the medicine man had merely to expunge the snake spirit that was causing the illness and to induce his patient to vomit up the spoiled saliva.

The Black Snake mentioned above is a spirit who is called upon to expel the disease-causing snake spirit. The Two Little Men are Thunder's sons, who were thought to be completely comfortable with snakes, and who could be called upon to aid men in time of troubles. The medicine man calls upon them to come and take the offending snake spirit away to the west, and there to put in into a black box or coffin. As soon as the Two Little Men turn around to face east, after having deposited the snake spirit in a black box, relief would be felt by the patient.

As the medicine man recited this formula, he rubbed upon his patient's body a syrup made from the root of rattlesnake fern (*Botrychium virginianum* (L.)). Then he blew his breath four times on the affected part of his patient's body. This entire ceremony was repeated four times, and then the patient drank a small amount of the syrup. The medicine man performed the first ceremony soon after sunrise, and the last one at about noon.

This syrup was an emetic. Once the spoiled saliva was expelled, and the snake spirit exorcized, the patient was placed into seclusion for four days.

If this procedure did not relieve the patient's symptoms, then the medicine man might conclude that his patient was suffering from a far more serious illness. He might, in fact, have had his saliva spoiled by a witch or a sorcerer. In this event, the medicine man would treat his patient further.

CHEROKEE DIVINATION

As we have seen, when people fell ill, the Cherokees heaped up ashes and coals into a mound and sprinkled pulverized tobacco leaves on it as a way of discovering the presence of witches. But this was only one of several means of divining into hidden causes and into the unknown.[16]

As a way of discovering the location of lost objects, or even lost people, they would tie a small lump of red ochre onto a string 25 to 30 cm long. They held the string between the thumb and index finger of the right hand while holding the left hand in front of the right one. A formula was recited extolling the acute vision and veracity of red ochre, which never fails to see and tell the truth. (One suspects that red ochre was used during Mississippian period to paint the V-shaped peregrine falcon eye pattern). Then, the pendulum would begin to swing, slowly at first, gradually gaining momentum. The direction in which the pendulum swung indicated the direction of the lost thing or person.

This same red ochre pendulum could be used to prognosticate whether a person would live or die. To do this, a piece of cloth some 10 cm by 10 cm was placed on the ground. The red ochre pendulum was placed on the center of the cloth. Then the diviner placed a lump of charcoal on the side of the cloth nearest him, and on the opposite side a piece of bread. The diviner then picked up the string, and if the pendulum swung first towards the

---

[16] Frans M. Olbrechts, "Some Cherokee Methods of Divination", *Proceedings of the Twenty-Third Congress of Americanists* (New York, 1930), 547-552.

bread, it indicat____ ___at the person would live, but if it first swung toward the black charcoal, it indic__ ___ death.

The Cherokees ____essed certain crystals into which they could gaze and prognosticate the future (Pl. XI___ ____ The most powerful of these was the u·*lahsathi* crystal, which was believed to be the _____ that blazed on the *uktena*'s forehead. When a question was addressed to it, it wa____ ___to either fill up with a white fluid (a good sign), or else a red fluid (a bad sign). The _____athi* was consulted in matters of grave importance, as when a war party was about t____ ___ut on a raid.

Another favorit_ ___erokee technique was divination with beads (Pl. XLII b). For example, if a man ____ ___ied to know whether he had succeeded in winning a particular woman's affection___ ___ might engage a medicine man to divine with beads. The medicine man would hold a l____k bead between the thumb and index finger of his left hand, and he held either a white __ _ed bead between the thumb and index finger of his right hand. He uttered a formula, and the beads would begin to move. James Mooney was never sure about whether the movement of the beads was caused by voluntary or involuntary muscular movements in the medicine man's fingers. If the left-hand bead showed vitality, the divination was favorable; if it was sluggish in its movements, the divination was unfavorable.

The Cherokees used yet another means of divination upon the occurrence of a new moon. An entire family would go with a medicine man to the Long Man—to the edge of a river. As they stood on the bank staring intently into the water, the medicine man recited a formula asking for long life for all the members of the family. If nothing floated into view, it meant that all could expect to live another seven years. But if anything floated into view—a leaf, a twig, or even if a fish broke the surface of the water—it meant that death or misfortune would ensue.

THE GREEN CORN CEREMONY

In addition to the ceremonies which Southeastern Indians performed at crucial junctures in the lives of individuals, such as rites of passage and treatment for illnesses, they also performed ceremonies on behalf of entire communities and chiefdoms. Before the arrival of Europeans, the Southeastern Indians appear to have performed an extensive series of ceremonials throughout the year, but only one of these remained vital into the nineteenth century, and it is performed in an attenuated way even to the present day—the Green Corn Ceremony (Pl. XLIII).

As its name implies the Green Corn Ceremony was celebrated when the new crop of green corn, or maize, had matured enough to be eaten, so that the time when it was celebrated could be any time from June to early September. Everywhere the Green Corn Ceremony was celebrated it was a rite of thanksgiving that the new crop was successful, but it was more than a mere first fruits ceremony. Just as there were ceremonies in which an individual could purify himself, the Green Corn Ceremony was the means by which the entire society could purify itself.

Representatives of all of a group of towns celebrating a Green Corn Ceremony would assemble and decide upon a date on which the ceremony would begin. They would then prepare a number of identical bundles of little sticks, about four inches long, one stick for each day until the ceremony was scheduled to begin. Runners would then go to the various towns and deliver a bundle of sticks to each. The chief of the town would then discard one stick each day, until only one remained. Then all of the people from the various towns would assemble at the ceremonial center where the rite was to be performed.

When they assembled, they ate a great quantity of food, in preparation for fasting, but they were careful to eat none of the fruits from the new crop. Then they refurbished and renewed all of the buildings at the square ground, their summer ceremonial center. The hearth in the center of the square ground was rebuilt, and they swept the place clean and spread down a layer of dirt or sand over the ground, and no one was permitted to walk upon it until the ceremony began. The square ground was very likely a microcosm of the world, so that in this act of refurbishing they symbolically made the earth anew, obliterating all traces of the previous year.

While the men were refurbishing the square ground, women cleaned and refurbished their households. They renewed their hearths and made new cooking vessels. A strict rule of avoidance was imposed between the sexes. A man could not touch even a female infant for the duration of the Green Corn Ceremony, thus underscoring what was the most fundamental social distinction in Southeastern Indian society, the difference between the sexes.

In the next episode in the ceremony, the men fasted for a day and two nights, repeatedly drinking a bitter emetic made of an herb, button snakeroot. It was during this time that the men discussed social conflicts and crimes of the previous year. Many of them were resolved at this time, and most of the people who had been expelled from society could return forgiven.

Tuckabahchee, an important Upper Creek town, had an episode in its Green Corn Ceremony which may have been a remnant of Mississippian ceremonialism. That is, at one point in the ceremony they brought out and displayed a number of objects made of copper and brass. Some were circular plates, while others were cut in the shape of celts or war axes. The brass articles were definitely acquired from Europeans, but the copper ones could have been made from native copper. Women were forbidden to see these objects. The objects were taken down to a river or creek, where they were ceremonially washed and scoured until they shone in the sunlight. Then they were taken to the square ground where they were displayed on a bed of white sand. Later they were returned to the place where they were kept.

The men who had been fasting ate some food, and then one or several of the medicine men performed one of the most crucial acts in the ceremony—the making of new fire. All fires everywhere were extinguished. And when the time came to kindle new fires, everyone fell absolutely silent while a priest created fire by friction, using a fire drill. When it ignited, a large fire in the center of the ceremonial ground was built, and from this fire everyone came and took fire to their houses. One of the priests gave some of the new fruits to the fire and poured in some black drink and button snakeroot medicine. This marked the true beginning of a new year. All crimes except homicide were forgiven (and in principle, forgotten), and everything started afresh.

At this point the women were called out of their houses. They appeared dressed in finery, and they danced their own dance in the ceremonial ground, some with terrapin shell rattles attached to their legs.

Next the men drank black drink brewed from the parched leaves of *Ilex vomitoria*. This was their main social beverage. It contained caffeine, and hence it was comparable to tea or coffee in our own culture. But they drank it more ceremoniously than we, out of large conchshell cups or out of gourds which had been painted white. They sometimes vomited after drinking black drink, but their doing so appears to have somehow been a voluntary act, because in and of itself, black drink is not an emetic (Pl. XLIV a and b).

The Green Corn Ceremony ended with feasting on the new fruits, dancing, mock fighting by the warriors, games, and at the very end all went to a river or creek, immersed themselves, and came out purified for a new year of social life. The Green Corn Ceremony was a ritual turning point of great importance. It was as if the entire social fabric was dusted off, tidied up, and set in order.

Missionaries and Prophets

The separate existence of the Southeastern Indians came to an end with the arrival of the first Spanish explorers in the sixteenth century. During the three centuries which followed, the Southeastern Indians were to lose first their autonomy, and then their land, and finally they lost most of their culture. Hence, after the arrival of Europeans, the Southeastern Indians became engaged in an ideological struggle as well as an economic and political struggle.

The first concerted missionary effort among the Southeastern Indians was organized by the Spanish. Beginning in 1566 the Jesuits established a number of precarious missions along the coasts of present Florida, Georgia, and South Carolina. But some of these Jesuit missionaries died of illness, and others were killed by Indians, and having failed to establish an effective mission system, the rest were withdrawn. The next order to try was the Franciscans, and beginning in 1583, and using a new approach, they succeeded in building a mission system. They taught the Indians in their missions Catholic dogma, and they taught them to speak Spanish. They persuaded and coerced as many Indians as they could to settle in larger villages and to cultivate grains, vegetables, and fruits which could be used to feed themselves and their Spanish masters.

Gradually the Francisicans built a series of missions in northern Florida, along the Georgia coast, and in northwest Florida (Pl. XLV a and b). The missions in northwest Florida were especially important, because this area became the bread basket of Spanish Florida. In their missions the Franciscan priests would assemble the Indians for devotionals each morning. Then they would send them to the fields to labor, and finally they would end the day with prayers, which the Indians learned by rote.

The Franciscans attempted to supplant the Indian's world view with their own. The degree to which they were successful is unknown. It is, however, clear that by the middle of the seventeenth century the Franciscans were as interested in having the Indians serve them as a docile labor force as they were in proselytizing. For the most part, the Spanish did not meddle in the affairs of the Indians in the interior of the Southeast, and only minimal amounts of Spanish trade goods reached them. The only occasions in which the Spanish became interested in the Indians in the interrior was when they perceived a threat from French and British colonial activity.

Spain was not destined to win the hearts and minds of the Southeastern Indians. This was to be the achievement of the British, who proceeded by first winning the economic interests of the Indians, with the assumption that their hearts and minds would follow. That is, the English succeeded in winning the Southeast through an aggressive trading policy by means of which they succeeded in bringing the Indians into economic dependency. By this device, they were able to gain political control over the Indians. Indeed, together with a large force of Indian mercenaries, the English colonists in South Carolina were able to completely destroy the Spanish mission system within the space of about twenty years. Many of the Indians who were displaced from these missions—Spanish-speaking and nominally Catholic—were enslaved and put to work on plantations.

After the founding of the South Carolina colony in 1670, English traders succeeded in penetrating all the way to the Mississippi River by 1698. But one flaw in the English system was that the traders often abused the Indians and took advantage of them. In time this led to two large-scale Indian wars which dealt heavy blows against the colonists. The first was the Tuscarora war which broke out in 1711. Then followed the far bigger and more serious Yamasee war in 1715, in which many different groups of Southeastern Indians cooperated in a determined attack against the South Carolina colonists. Thousands of Creeks, Choctaws, Yamasees, Cherokees, and others went into the fray, and they very nearly succeeded in crushing the colony. Characteristically though, after winning an initial advantage, the Indians failed to push their actions to a full military victory, and within a few years were again under the yoke of the traders.

The Yamasee war was planned by the Indians with such secrecy that hardly anything is known of the thinking which lay behind it. It is clear that the war was an action against the excesses of the Carolina trading regime, because the first to be killed were the traders. Because such large numbers of warriors were mobilized in the Yamasee war, it is likely that it was impelled by a prophetic or millenarian movement of the kind which has occurred in many parts of the colonial world. Such movements occur in simple societies when people realize that basic changes are being forced upon them and that their fortunes are sinking. Typically, in such situations prophets arise who promise that if certain drastic measures be taken, the old order can be reinstated.

Clearly this is what happened in the Creek wars of 1813-1814.[17] The Upper Creek Indians lived in present Alabama along the lower courses of the Coosa and Tallapoosa Rivers and along the upper Alabama River. This was a favorable location throughout the eighteenth century because it was so far inland it could not easily be attacked by British, Spanish, or French forces. But in the years following the American Revolution, after all of the major European powers had been eliminated, the Creeks came face to face with American frontiersmen and farmers, whose population was burgeoning and whose desire for land knew no limit. Other Indians in the Southeast were at this time being forced to cede lands to the Americans, and the Creeks knew it. In 1805 some Creek chiefs granted the Americans permission to build a road through their territory. As traffic along this road increased, the Creeks became uneasy as they faced a future that seemed more and more uncertain.

It was in this atmosphere of anger and anxiety that the Shawnee war chief Tecumseh appeared among the Creeks in the fall of 1811. Tecumseh, claiming supernatural

---

[17] Theron A. Nunez, Jr., "Creek Nativism and the Creek War of 1813-1814", *Ethnohistory* 5(1958):1-41, 131-175, 292-301.

guidance, was trying to unite Indians from the Great Lakes to the Gulf of Mexico to stand in a united front against the Americans. He admonished the Indians to return to their old ways, to cast aside their European goods, to throw away their plows and looms, their European clothing, and to take up the warclub and knife. Tecumseh promised to give the Creeks a sign of his power. He told them that he would return north to his people, where he would perform a ritual, and then he would ascend a high mountain. Here he would stamp his foot, and the entire earth would tremble.

As it so happened, about three months after he departed an earthquake occurred which was felt by the Creeks. These events only inflamed an already volatile situation, and a number of prophets, most of whom were of mixed white-Indian ancestry, arose among the Creeks promising divinely inspired solutions to their problems.

One of these, the prophet Francis (also called Hillis Hadjo, "Crazy Medicine"), told his followers that Master of Breath, the Creek deity, had instructed him in the art of understanding and writing European languages. He composed a long letter to the commander of the Spanish garrison at Pensacola requesting arms and ammunition so that he could wage war against the Americans. He sent a party of his men to carry it to Pensacola. When the Spanish commander read it, it was only marks on paper. The commander is said to have laughed, saying that he should send the prophet Francis a reply in kind.

Francis was next inspired to build a sacred town which he promised to surround with a magical barrier through which a white man could not pass alive. The town was named Ecanachaga—"sacred or beloved ground." However, not long after it was built an army of volunteers under General Ferdinand Claiborne successfully crossed the barrier and routed the town. Francis and many of his followers fled south to join the British.

Another prophet, Paddy Walsh, son of a South Carolina Tory and a Creek woman, sought a solution to Creek problems through military actions. He and other prophets led the Creeks in an attack on Fort Mims, a small, crudely built fort in lower Alabama. He convinced four of his men that he had made them invulnerable to white men's bullets, and he sent them running into the fort through a gate which carelessly had been left open. They expected to kill many of their enemies. But immediately upon entering, three of them were killed; the fourth turned on his heels and ran back unharmed. Next Paddy promised that he himself would run around the fort three times, and after doing this the bullets of the defenders would drop harmlessly from their guns, or else go straight up in the air. He started running his circuits, but on one of them he was wounded. Eventually, the Creek warriors succeeded in taking the fort and in killing almost everyone inside, but they lost many of their own warriors in the attack.

Though these Creek prophets failed to achieve what they claimed to be able to achieve, the very fact that they were able to mobilize such large numbers of committed followers shows that a native Creek belief system was still very much alive in 1813-14. In time, the prophets and their Creek warriors were defeated by Andrew Jackson, and they were then forced to cede an immense portion of their land to the Americans. The prophets were discredited, and the credibility of their native world view must have been seriously weakened.

The Creeks were not the only Indians in the Southeast who remained outside the pale of Christianity until the early years of the nineteenth century. They were able to do so because the British had relatively little interest in missionizing the Southeastern Indians. The Anglicans sent missionaries to work with the Indians early in the eighteenth century, and the Methodists John and Charles Wesley tried to win Indian souls in the 1730s. But their efforts came to very little. The Moravians established a mission and school in Georgia in 1737, and it enjoyed some success, but it was abandoned when the Moravians departed from Georgia after a political disagreement.[18]

It was after the war of 1812, during both a nationalistic and religious fervor in America, that various Protestant organizations became interested in missionizing the Southeastern Indians. With hardly any exceptions, these missionaries were from northern states. In the South, pressure was mounting to "remove" the Indians and open up their lands for speculation and agriculture. Few Southerners wanted to missionize or "civilize" the Indians. Indeed, part of the rhetoric in the southern states in favor of removal was that the Indians were uncivilized, savage hunters who could not make good use of their land.

In 1801 the Moravians established a successful mission among the Cherokees at Spring Place in northern Georgia. In 1818 the American Board of Commissioners for Foreign Missions established another mission among the Cherokees—the Brainerd Mission—near Chattanooga, Tennessee. Also in 1818, the Presbyterians established a mission among the Choctaws. Other missions were established, with mixed success, among the Creeks and Chickasaws.

One strategy of these missionaries was to build schools to inculcate their beliefs into the Indian children (Pl. XLVI a and b). They taught them reading and writing, and certain manual skills, as well as teaching them about Christianity. In general, the Indians who were of mixed white-Indian parentage were the ones who took to these missions and schools most enthusiastically.

In addition to inculcating school children with Christianity, the missionaries attempted to work changes in Indian adults by opposing certain native institutions and practices. For example, the missionaries opposed plural marriage, and of course they attempted to dissuade the Indians from consulting with "conjurers" or "medicine men". They were also opposed to the stickball game, to which the Southeastern Indians were passionately devoted. Stickball games were the occasion of much gambling and fighting, and the missionaries realized that stickball games were accompanied by elaborate native rituals.

At the very time these Protestant missionaries began working with the Southeastern Indians for the purpose of Christianizing and "civilizing" them, the pressure for their removal from their homeland began to increase. The Choctaws were the first to be removed. Some of them departed for Oklahoma in late 1830, and others followed. Then, systematically, the other Southeastern Indians were removed. Only the Seminoles in Florida resisted militarily, but at last they too were defeated. In 1842 most of the Seminoles were removed to Oklahoma, leaving only a handful who never surrendered.

In addition to these few Seminoles who were able to remain in their native Southeast, so too did a few Choctaws, Cherokees, and Catawbas evade removal. But whether these Southeastern Indians lived in the Southeast or in Oklahoma, the erosion of their culture

---

[18] Karen G. Wood. "Nineteenth Century Missions among the Southeastern Indians", manuscript.

continued through the efforts of the missionaries and educators, and also because they were participating more and more in American society.

Belief systems do not suddenly die and become extinct, like passenger pigeons or Carolina parakeets. And we possess no precise way of speaking about relative decline in the integrity of belief systems, nor of their "hold" upon the minds of people. But it is clear that no prophets ever again arose who possessed the moral force of the Creek prophets of the early nineteenth century. Also, as the nineteenth century progressed, most of the Southeastern Indians, whether in the Southeast itself or in Oklahoma, became members of various Protestant churches.

But it is also clear that even though the Southeastern Indians became members of Baptist, Methodist, Presbyterian, and other Protestant churches, many of them still believed in parts of the old belief system which still survived. It was still possible in the late nineteenth and early twentieth centuries for conservative Indians to form organizations which promised to promote spiritual betterment by a return to old beliefs and ritual forms. This was the case with the Cherokee Keetoowa society, and particularly the form it took under the leadership of Redbird Smith (Pl. XLVII). Most of the people who were involved in these movements were Christians; they saw no contradiction between going to church on Sunday and later in the week consulting a medicine man about some matter for which Christianity had no ready solution.

In some places some of the old ritual forms are preserved to the present day. Many Southeastern Indians attend "stomp dances", though these are mostly pan-Indian in form. A few still play the old stickball game, though in most cases the games are "enactments" for tourists and spectators who buy tickets to see the games (Pl. XLVIII a and b). A few Southeastern groups, such as the Yuchis, still perform a Green Corn Ceremony which still retains many traditional symbolic forms, even though it lacks the religious significance it once had, when time stopped, and then started, and the world was made anew.

CATALOGUE OF ILLUSTRATIONS

Plates I to IX: Early Prehistory

Plate Ia:

Hammered repoussé copper plaque of opposed raptorial birds from Mound City, Ohio. Woodland period. Length 28 cm. Drawn by C. Hudson III.
Bibl. Willey, *An Introduction to American Archaeology*, p. 275, plate 5-24.

Plate Ib:

The "Wilmington tablet." Opposed raptorial birds on a carved and incised sandstone slab from Clinton County, Ohio. Woodland period. About 6 × 9 in. Drawn by C. Hudson III from Dockstader, *Indian Art in America*, pl. 25.
Bibl. Penny, "The Adena Engraved Tablets",p. 29.

Plate II:

Top and bottom views of a horned serpentine monster carved from slate (cannel coal) from a mound in the Turner group, Hamilton County, Ohio. Woodland period. Length about 24 cm. Drawn by C. Hudson III from Willoughby (1922), plate 19.
Bibl. Willey, *An Introduction to American Archaeology*, p. 277.

Plate III:

Circular and square earthworks near Chillicothe, Ohio. Woodland period. Author's photo.
Bibl. Squier and Davis, *Ancient Monuments of the Mississippi Valley*, pl. XX.

Plate IV:

Platform pipes from the Tunacunnhee site in northwestern Georgia. Upper left: sandstone plain monitor pipe. Upper right: polished rhyolite porphyry monitor pipe. Center: sandstone pipe in the form of an alligator snapping turtle. Lower left: sandstone pipe in the form of a raptorial bird. Lower right: tubular pipe in the form of a snail. Photo courtesy of the Laboratory of Archaeology, University of Georgia.
Bibl. Jeffries, *The Tunacunnhee Site*, pl. 19.

Plate Va:

Mica head ornament, probably representing a feather. 5.4 × 2.8 in. Woodland period. Photograph courtesy of Laboratory of Archaeology, University of Georgia.
Bibl. Jeffries, *The Tunacunnhee Site*, pl. 20.

Plate Vb:

Copper breast plate. 9 × 4.5 in. Woodland period. Photograph courtesy of Laboratory of Archaeology, University of Georgia.
Bibl. Jeffries, *The Tunacunnhee Site*, pl. 17.

Plate VIa:

Burial mounds surrounded by an earthen enclosure at the Mound City site, in Ross County, Ohio. Woodland period. Author's photograph.
Bibl. Squier and Davis, *Ancient Mounds of the Mississippi Valley*, pl. XIX.

Plate VIb:

Burial of a Timucuan chief. His house was set on fire, and his conchshell drinking cup was placed atop the small mound over his grave. Engraved by Theodore de Bry after a painting by Jacques le Moyne de Morgues, 1564-65. Courtesy Smithsonian Institution.
Bibl. Swanton, *The Indians of the Southeastern United States*, pl. 87.

Plate VII:

The Serpent Mound in Adams County, Ohio. Woodland period. Author's photo.
Bibl. Squier and Davis, *Ancient Mounds of the Mississippi Valley*, pl. XXXV.

Plate VIII:

Sixteenth century Algonkian mortuary practices. The bodies were defleshed. The seated figure at upper left was a wooden idol, Kiwasa. A priest at lower right tends a fire. Theodore de Bry engraving after a John White watercolor. Author's photo.
Bibl. Harriot, *A Briefe and True Report of the New Found Land of Virginia*, pl. XXII.

Plate IX:

Masks of Indians of south Florida. Above: two-part wolf mask. Below: two-part pelican mask. Both are from Key Marco, c. 1500. Author's photo.
Bibl. Cushing, *A Preliminary Report on the Exploration of Ancient Key-Dweller Remains on the Gulf Coast of Florida*, pl. XXXIII; Gilliland, *The Material Culture of Key Marco, Florida*, pls. 49, 54, 64 and 67.

Plates X to XXXIV: Late Prehistory—The Southeastern Ceremonial Complex

Plate X:

Variants of Southeastern Ceremonial Complex motifs. I. Cross. II. Sun circle. III. Bilobed arrow. IV. Forked eye. V. Open eye. VI. Barred oval. VII. Hand and eye. VIII. Death motifs. Author's photo, permission of the American Anthropological Association.
Bibl. Waring and Holder, "A Prehistoric Ceremonial Complex", Fig. I.

Plate XI:

Southeastern Ceremonial Complex ritual objects. a-e: embossed copper plates. f-j: monolithic stone axes. k: hafted copper celt in the form of a woodpecker, with beak open and tongue extruded. l-w: batons [i.e., war clubs]. x-z: copper symbol badges in the shape of stylized feathers. Author's photo, permission of the American Anthropological Association.

Bibl. Waring and Holder, "A Prehistoric Ceremonial Complex", Fig. II.

Plate XII:

Southeastern Ceremonial Complex ritual objects. a: ceremonial flints from Tennessee and Georgia. b-c: simple circular shell gorgets. d-e: mask gorgets. f-g: copper covered ear-spools of stone. h-j: tripartite bottles. k-l: painted bottles with cross and sun circle. m-o: oblong gorgets of copper [representing scalp-locks]. p-q: circular gorgets of copper. r-s: columnella pendants. t-v: engraved stone discs. Author's photo, permission of the American Anthropological Association.

Bibl. Waring and Holder, "A Prehistoric Ceremonial Complex." Fig. III.

Plate XIII:

Southeastern Ceremonial Complex god-animal representations. a-c: embossed copper plates of the [falcon]. d: [falcon] being anthropomorphized. e-i: woodpecker. j: one of the wilder variations from Spiro [i.e., anomalous serpent]. k: bird-serpent composite. l: anthropomorphized and naturalistic serpent representations. Author's photo, by permission of the American Anthropological Association.

Bibl. Waring and Holder, "A Prehistoric Ceremonial Complex", Fig. IV.

Plate XIV:

Southeastern Ceremonial Complex god-animal representations. a, b, c, and f: variations of the anthropomorphized [falcon] being from Etowah and Spiro. d, e, g, h, and i: representations from Spiro. Author's photo, by permission of the American Anthropological Association.

Bibl. Waring and Holder, "A Prehistoric Ceremonial Complex", Fig. V.

Plate XVa:

Sixteenth century Timucuan Indians planting maize and beans. The men tilled the earth with short hoes, and the women planted the seeds. The picture errs in showing rows; the Indians planted in "hills", or little mounds of soil. Engraving by Theodore de Bry after a painting by Jacques le Moyne de Morgues, 1564-65. Courtesy Smithsonian Institution.

Bibl. Lorant, *The New World*, p. 77.

Plate XVb:

Early spring ritual of sixteenth century Timucuan Indians. As an offering to the sun, they hung up a deerskin which had been stuffed with wild edible roots and festooned with wild fruits. Hence, it was probably a hunting and gathering ritual. Engraving by Theodore de Bry after a painting by Jacques le Moyne de Morgues, 1564-65. Courtesy Smithsonian Institution.

Bibl. Swanton, *The Indians of the Southeastern United States*, p. 97.

Plate XVI:

The Moundville site on the Black Warrior River in Alabama, a large Mississippian site. Author's photo.
Bibl. Moore, "Moundville Revisited", frontispiece.

Plate XVIIa:

Some of the mounds at the Moundville site. Foreground: mound A as seen from atop mound B. Background, from right to left: mounds L, K, J, I, and T. Author's photo.

Plate XVIIb:

Mound and reconstructed temple at the Town Creek site near Mt. Gilead, N.C., a small Mississippian site. Author's photo.

Plate XVIIIa:

Reconstructed log palisade surrounding the Town Creek site. Author's photo.

Plate XVIIIb:

Reconstructed defensive tower and gate at the Town Creek site. Author's photo.

Plate XIXa:

Circular stone tablet from Etowah, a Mississippian site in Georgia. Diameter 12 in. Photo courtesy Georgia Department of Natural Resources.

Plate XIXb:

Circular common dance of the Natchez Indians, early eighteenth century. Males with gourd rattles form the outer circle, females the inner circle, and a drummer is in the center. Author's photo.
Bibl. Du Pratz, *Histoire de la Louisiane*, Vol. 2, pl. opposite p. 376.

Plate XXa:

Map of an eighteenth century Creek town showing the square ground or summer council house (B) in relation to the circular winter council house (A), and to a plaza or commons (C). These are surrounded by houses and fenced garden plots. Author's photo.
Bibl. Bartram, "Observations on the Creek and Cherokee Indians, 1780", Fig. 4.

Plate XXb:

Council house of the Alabama Indians, i.e. one of the four cabins forming their square ground. Note the pots and conchshell cups for black drink and other "medicines." Probably early eighteenth century. Photo courtesy Smithsonian Institution.
Bibl. Swanton, *Social Organization and Social Usages of the Indians of the Creek Confederacy*, Fig. 5.

Plate XXI:

Left and right: Mississippian chipped flint replicas of wooden war clubs. Photo courtesy the Thruston Collection, Tennessee State Museum.

Plate XXIIa:

Mississippian bowmen incised on a shell cup from Spiro, Oklahoma. Redrawn by C. Hudson III.
Bibl. Phillips and Brown, *Pre-Columbian Shell Engravings*, Fig. 141.

Plate XXIIb:

Natchez warrior in summer dress armed with a war club and bow and arrows. Early eighteenth century. Author's photo.
Bibl. Du Pratz, *Histoire de la Louisiane*, Vol. 2, p. 308.

Plate XXIIIa:

Shell gorget showing a warrior with a war club and a human head. Note the falcon eye marking, beaded forelock, bi-lobed arrow, and pointed pouch. Castalian Springs site, Tennessee. Drawn by C. Hudson III.
Bibl. Dockstader, *Indian Art in America*, pl. 64.

Plate XXIIIb:

Broken war clubs and severed heads. Incised on a Spiro conchshell cup. Redrawn by C. Hudson III.
Bibl. Phillips and Brown, *Pre-Columbian Shell Engravings*, pl. 55.

Plate XXIVa:

Possible representation of Mississippian torture or sacrifice. Incised on a conchshell cup from Spiro, Oklahoma. Redrawn by C. Hudson III.
Bibl. Phillips and Brown, *Pre-Columbian Shell Engravings*, Fig. 143.

Plate XXIVb:

Natchez Indians torturing a war captive in a frame and scalping another. Early eighteenth century. Author's photo.
Bibl. Du Pratz, *Histoire de la Louisiane*, Vol. 2, opp. p. 429.

Plate XXVa:

Mississippian high status burial from Tennessee. Especially noteworthy are the ceramic bottle, stone celt, and two large conchshell cups. Photo courtesy of Richard Polhemus, Frank H. McClung Museum, University of Tennessee.

Plate XXVb:

Mortuary ceremony of the Natchez war leader, Tattooed-Serpent. The corpse is shown being carried on a litter on the shoulders of bearers who moved in clockwise circles. Eight retainers are shown being strangled to death; their bodies were buried along with that of Tattooed-Serpent. Early eighteenth century. Courtesy Smithsonian Institution.

Bibl. Du Pratz, *Histoire de la Louisiane*, Vol. 3, opposite p. 55.

Plate XXVIa:

Mississippian chunkey stone from the King site, Georgia. Photo courtesy Laboratory of Archaeology, University of Georgia.

Plate XXVIb:

Mississippian shell gorget showing a player casting a chunkey stone. Found at Eddyville, Ky. Author's photo.

Bibl. MacCurdy, "Shell Gorgets from Missouri", p. 406.

Plate XXVIc:

Mandan Indians playing chunkey. Drawing by George Catlin, 1832. Author's photo.

Bibl. Catlin, *Letters and Notes on the Manners, Customs, and Conditions of the North American Indians*, Vol. I, pl. 59.

Plate XXVIIa:

Peregrine falcon (*Falco peregrinus*). Author's photo.

Bibl. Wilson, *American Ornithology*, p. 76.

Plate XXVIIb:

Drawing of a falcon dancer from a repousse copper plate found at the Etowah site, Georgia. Author's photo.

Bibl. Willoughby, "History and Symbolism of the Muskhogeans", Fig. 14, p. 34.

Plate XXVIIIa:

Wooden statue of anthropomorphized cougar from Key Marco. Height 6 in. Courtesy Smithsonian Institution.

Bibl. Gilliland, *The Material Culture of Key Marco*, pls. 69-71.

Plate XXVIIIb:

Mississippian shell gorget with spider motif. Author's photo.

Bibl. Holmes, "Art in Shell of the Ancient Americans", opposite p. 288.

Plate XXIXa:

Wild turkey (*Meleagris gallopavo*). Author's photo.

Bibl. Wilson, *American Ornithology*, p. B9.

Plate XXIXb:

Wild turkeys incised on a conchshell cup from Spiro, Oklahoma. Redrawn by C. Hudson III.
Bibl. Phillips and Brown, *Pre-Columbian Shell Engravings*, p. 87.

Plate XXXa:

Ivory-billed woodpecker (*Campephilus principalis*). Author's photo.
Bibl. Wilson, *American Ornithology*, p. 29.

Plate XXXb:

Mississippian shell gorget with woodpecker motif. Author's photo.
Bibl. Holmes, "Art in Shell of the Ancient Americans", opposite p. 282.

Plate XXXIa:

Raccoons incised on a conchshell cup from Spiro, Oklahoma. Redrawn by C. Hudson III.
Bibl. Phillips and Brown, *Pre-Columbian Shell Engravings*, Fig. 195.

Plate XXXIb:

Anomalous cougar with serpentine elements and a human head. Incised on a conch-shell cup from Spiro. Redrawn by C. Hudson III.
Bibl. Phillips and Brown, *Pre-Columbian Shell Engravings*, Fig. 207.

Plate XXXIIa:

Diamondback rattlesnake. Author's photo.

Plate XXXIIb:

Horned rattlesnakes and hand-and eye motif incised on a stone disc, Moundville, Alabama. Author's photo.

Plate XXXIIIa:

Winged horned serpent. Drawing taken from a design incised on a pot from Mound-ville, Alabama. Author's photo.
Bibl. Moore, "Moundville Revisited", Fig. 58, p. 374.

Plate XXXIIIb:

Anomalous rattlesnake gorget, McMahon Mound, Tennessee. The head is depicted with a huge, circular eye, and with an askew mouth filled with the teeth of an herbivore. The body of the serpent is coiled counterclockwise about the head, terminating with rattles. Author's photo.
Bibl. Holmes, "Art in Shell of the Ancient Americans", pl. LXIII.

Plate XXXIIIc:

Fantastic fish-deer incised on a conchshell cup from Spiro, Oklahoma. Redrawn by C. Hudson III.
Bibl. Phillips and Brown, *Pre-Columbian Shell Engravings*, pl. 92.

Plate XXXIVa:

Mississippian shell gorget from Spiro showing two men performing a ritual. Note the raccoon between them, as well as schematic raccoons hanging from their belts. Drawn by C. Hudson III.
Bibl. Fundaburk and Foreman, *Sun Circles and Human Hands*, pl. 23.

Plate XXXIVb:

Mississippian shell gorget showing two men performing a ritual. They appear to be stirring a pot full of steaming liquid. Drawn by C. Hudson III.
Bibl. Fundaburk and Foreman, *Sun Circles and Human Hands*, Fig. 28.

Plates XXXV to XXXIX: The Cherokee Cosmos

Plate XXXVa:

Swimmer. James Mooney's principal Cherokee informant. He holds a gourd rattle in his hand. Courtesy Smithsonian Institution.

Plate XXXVb:

A page from a Cherokee medicine man's book of sacred formulas. Courtesy Smithsonian Institution.

Plate XXXVI:

Stone statues from the Etowah site possibly representing archetypical man and woman. Left: male. Right: female. The square feature on the female's back may represent a schematic or symbolic infant on a cradleboard. Author's photo.

Plate XXXVIIa:

Mississippian vessel in the form of a fish, an underworld creature. Photo courtesy of the Thruston Collection, Tennessee State Museum.

Plate XXXVIIb:

Mississippian vessel in the form of a dog, a four-footed animal. Photo courtesy Laboratory of Archaeology, University of Georgia.

Plate XXXVIIc:

A bald eagle, supreme creature of the above. The Indians are Tomochichi (left), a Yamacraw chief of early Georgia, and Tooanahowi (right), his nephew. Engraving taken from a painting by Verelst, 1734. Permission of University of Georgia Library. Author's photo.

Plate XXXVIIIa:

Great horned owl (*Bubo virginianus*). Author's photo.
Bibl. Wilson, *American Ornithology*, p. 50.

Plate XXXVIIIb:

Mississippian pot in the form of a great horned owl. Photo courtesy Frank McClung Museum, University of Tennessee.

Plate XXXIXa:

Mississippian pot in the form of a bear, an anomalous animal. Photo courtesy Thruston Collection, Tennessee State Museum.

Plate XXXIXb:

Belted kingfisher (*Megaceryle alcyon*), an anomalous bird. Author's photo.
Bibl. Wilson, *American Ornithology*, p. 23.

Plate XXXIXc:

Mississippian shell gorget probably depicting the belted kingfisher. Drawn by C. Hudson III.
Bibl. Fundaburk and Foreman, *Sun Circles and Human Hands*, pl. 43.

Plates XL to XLI: Cherokee Curing

Plate XL:

Cherokee surgical instruments. d and i: the comb-like *kanuga*, a scratching instrument. a, b, and c: flint scratching instruments. e: blackberry briar. f: laurel (*Kalmia latifolia*) leaves, whose bristly edges were used for scratching. g: a sucking horn. h: a blowing tube, made from a section of trumpet weed (*Eupatorium purpureum*), used to spray or blow medicine on a patient's body. Courtesy Smithsoninan Institution.
Bibl. Olbrechts, *The Swimmer Manuscript*, pl. 7.

Plate XLIa:

Cherokee medicine man ritually scratching a stickball player before a game. Courtesy Smithsonian Institution.

Plate XLIb:

Cherokee medicine man collecting the root of an inverted raspberry branch for use as medicine. Photo by Franz Olbrechts in 1926 or 1927. Courtesy Smithsonian Institution.
Bibl. Olbrechts, *The Swimmer Manuscript*, pl. 6.

Plate XLII: Cherokee Divination

Plate XLIIa:

A Cherokee divining crystal. Collection of James H. Howard. Author's photo.

Plate XLIIb:

Cherokee method of holding beads for divination. Drawn by Frans Olbrechts. Author's photo.
Bibl. Kilpatrick and Kilpatrick, "Eastern Cherokee Folk Tales", p. 433.

Plates XLIII to XLIV: The Green Corn Ceremony

Plate XLIII:

Creek green corn ceremony. Museum diorama at Ocmulgee National Monument, Macon, Georgia. Author's photo.

Plate XLIVa:

Sprig of yaupon holly (*Ilex vomitoria*), the tree from whose parched leaves the Southeastern Indians brewed black drink. Drawing by Shiu Ying Hu. Author's photo.
Bibl. Hudson, *Black Drink*, Fig. 1.

Plate XLIVb:

Timucuan Indians drinking black drink. Some are vomiting. Theodore de Bry engraving after a painting by Jacques le Moyne de Morgues. Courtesy Smithsonian Institution.
Bibl. Swanton, *The Indians of the Southeastern United States*, pl. 98.

Plates XLV to XLVIII: Missionaries and Prophets

Plate XLVa:

Devils carrying away an Indian. Woodcut in Fr. Francisco Pareja's *Confessionario*, published in Spanish and Timucuan in 1613. Pareja was a Franciscan who missionized Indians in northern Florida and southeastern Georgia. The purpose of the woodcut may have been to frighten Indians into becoming converts. Permission Florida Divison of Archives, History, and Records Management.
Bibl. Milanich and Sturtevant, *Francisco Pareja's 1613 Confessionario*, p. 80.

Plate XLVb:

Artist's conception of San Juan de Aspalaga, a Spanish mission near Tallahassee, Florida which was built before 1647. Author's photo. Permission Florida Division of Archives, History, and Records Management.
Bibl. Morrell and Jones, "San Juan de Aspalaga", p. 42.

Plate XLVIa:

Samuel A. Worcester house and mission school at New Echota, Georgia. Worcester was an American Board missionary and teacher among the Cherokees in the early nineteenth century. Author's photo.

Plate XLVIb:

Reconstructed printing shop at New Echota, Georgia. Before removal, the Cherokees operated a printing press on this site. They published a newspaper, *The Cherokee Phoenix*, in Cherokee and English, as well as hymn books and religious tracts in Cherokee. Author's photo.

Plate XLVII:

Redbird Smith (second from left) and associates holding up wampum belts. Note the drum and crossed ballsticks in the foreground. Photograph taken about 1905. Courtesy of Robert K. Thomas.

Plate XLVIIIa:

Cherokee stickball dance. Photo by James Mooney in 1888. Courtesy of the Smithsonian Institution.

Plate XLVIIIb:

Cherokee stickball game, 1971. Cherokee players now play the game using only one ballstick. Author's photo.

PLATES

I b). The Wilmington tablet, Woodland period.

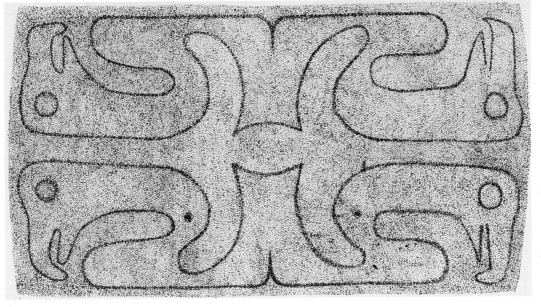

I a). Opposed raptorial birds, Woodland period.

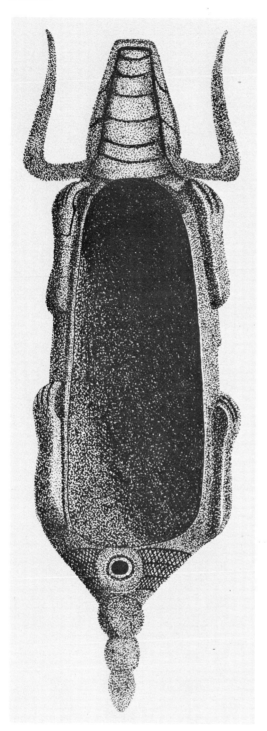 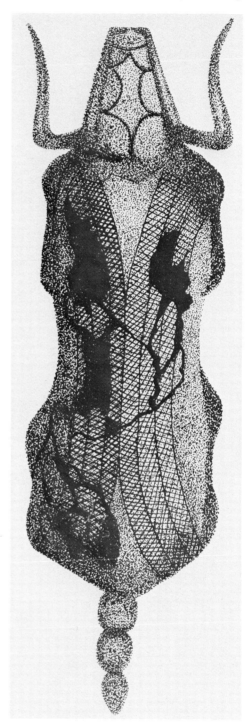

II. Horned serpentine monster, Woodland period.

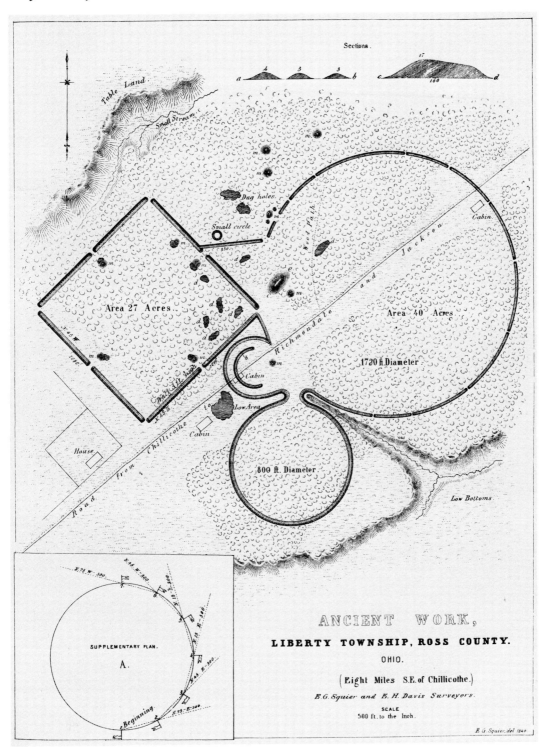

III. Woodland earthworks.

Plate IV   *Early Prehistory*

IV. Woodland platform pipes.

V a). Mica head ornament, Woodland period.

V b). Copper breast plate, Woodland period.

Plate VI   *Early Prehistory*

VI a). Woodland burial mounds and earthen enclosure.

VI b). Burial of a Timucuan chief.

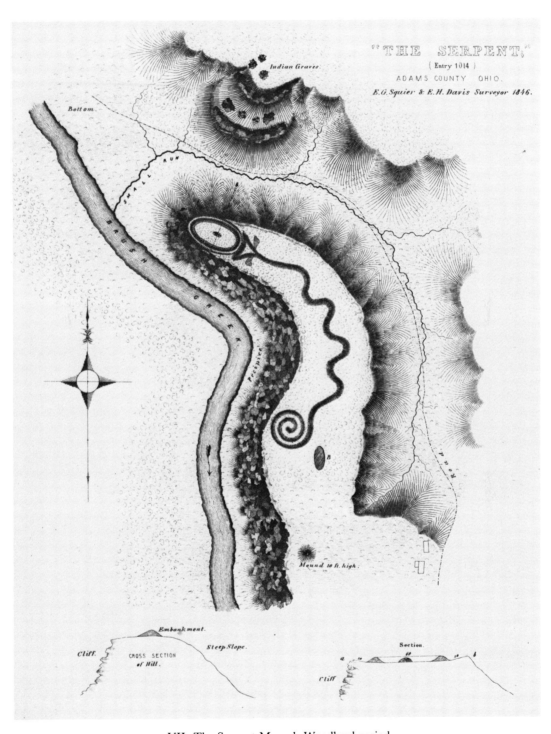

VII. The Serpent Mound, Woodland period.

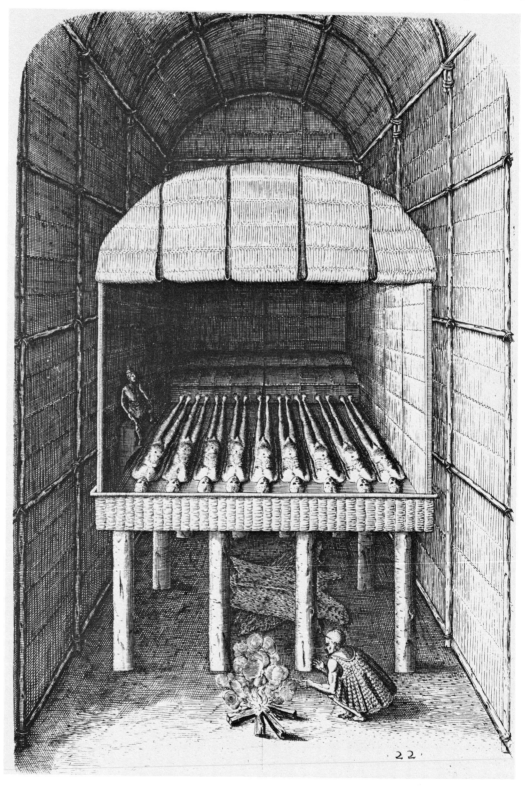

VIII. Algonkian mortuary practices, sixteenth century.

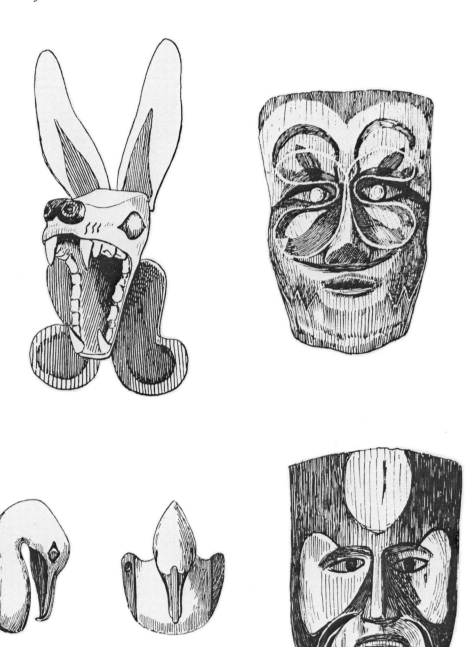

IX. Masks of Indians of south Florida.

Plate X   *Late Prehistory*

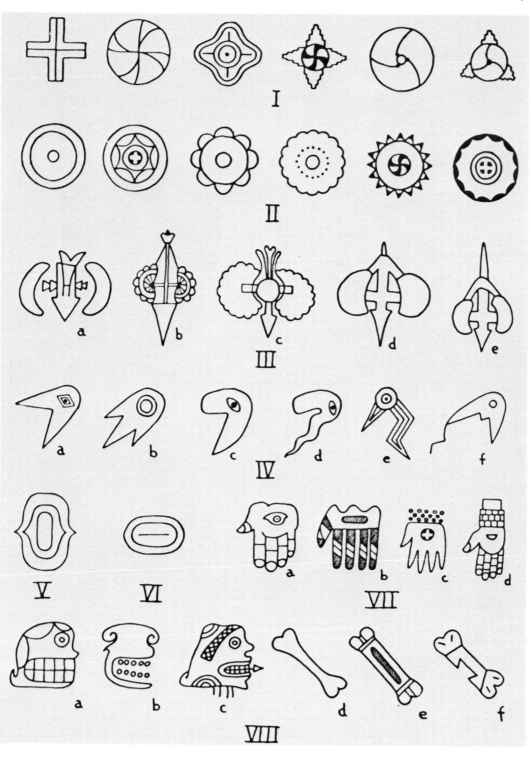

X. Southeastern Ceremonial Complex motifs.

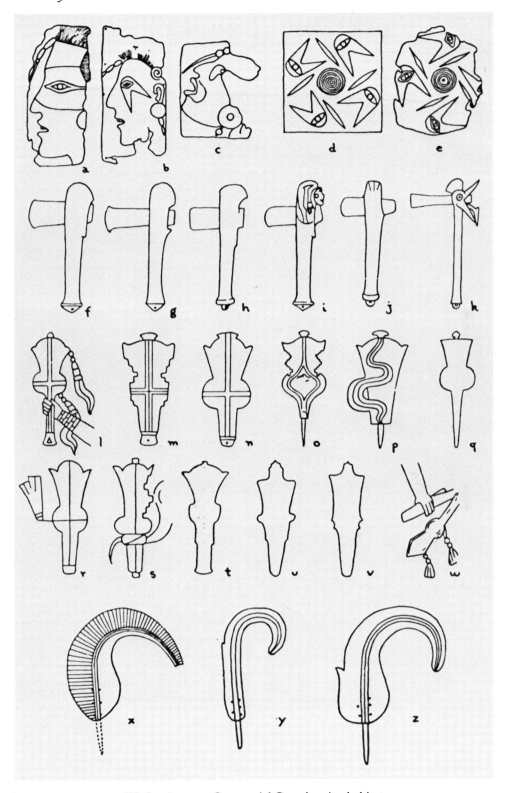

XI. Southeastern Ceremonial Complex ritual objects.

Plate XII

Late Prehistory

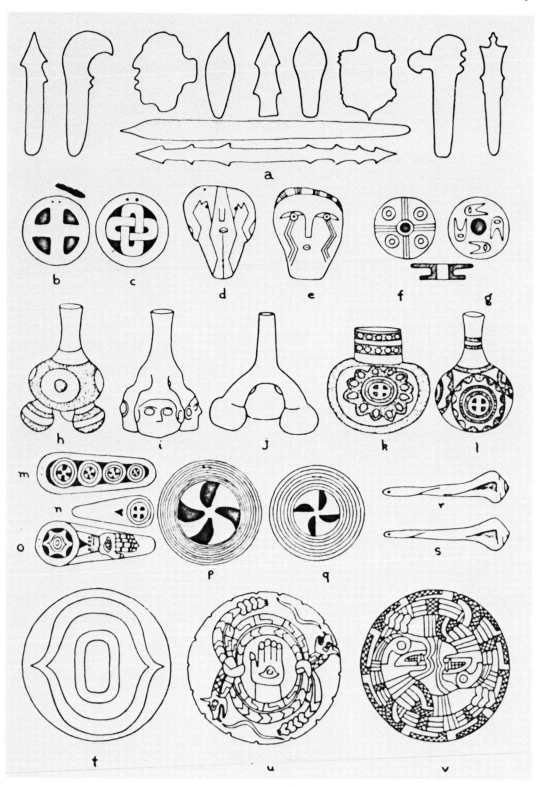

XII. Southeastern Ceremonial Complex ritual objects.

XIII. Southeastern Ceremonial Complex god-animal representations.

XIV. Southeastern Ceremonial Complex god-animal representations.

XV a). Timucuan Indians planting maize and beans.

XV b). Timucuan Indian early spring ritual.

Plate XVI   *Late Prehistory*

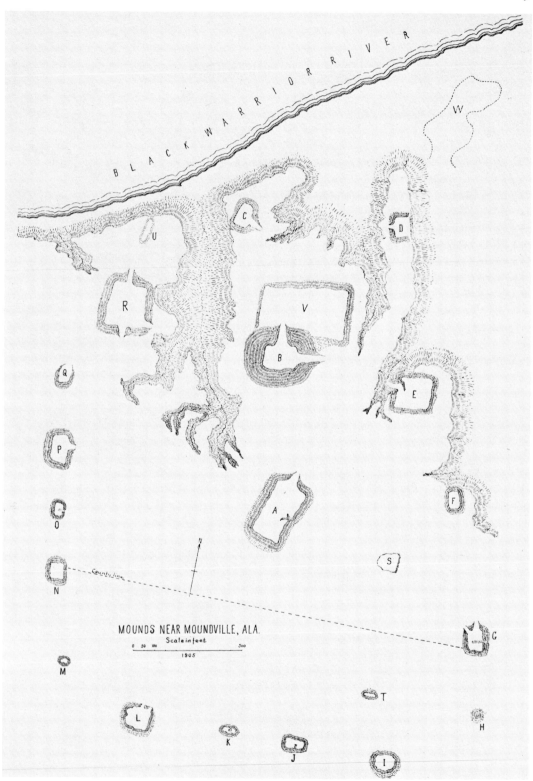

XVI. Moundville, a large Mississippian site.

XVII a). Some of the mounds at Moundville.

XVII b). Reconstructed temple at the Town Creek site.

Plate XVIII   *Late Prehistory*

XVIII a). Reconstructed log palisade, Town Creek.

XVIII b). Reconstructed defensive tower, Town Creek.

Dance générale.

XIX b). Circular dance of the Natchez Indians, early eighteenth century.

XIX a). Circular stone tablet, Etowah.

Plate XX   *Late Prehistory*

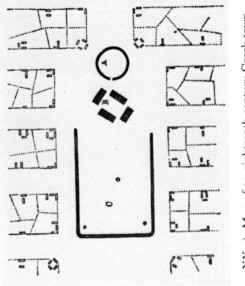

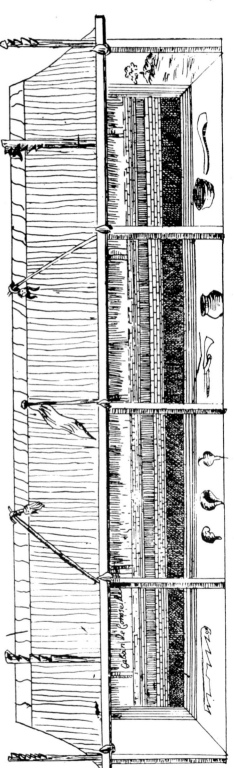

XX a). Map of an eighteenth century Creek town.

XXI. Mississippian flint replicas of war clubs.

Plate XXII *Late Prehistory*

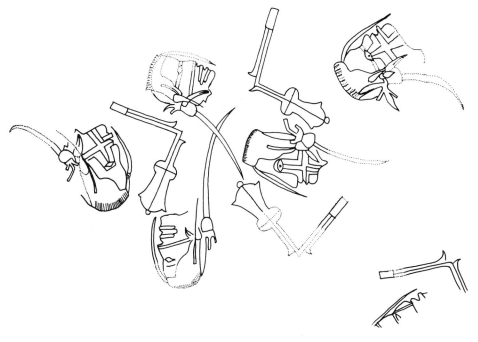

XXIII b). Broken war clubs and severed heads, Mississippian period.

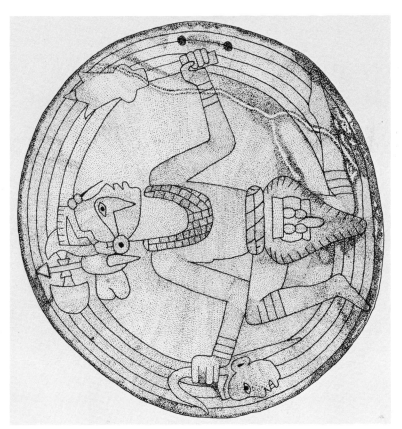

XXIII a). Mississippian warrior gorget.

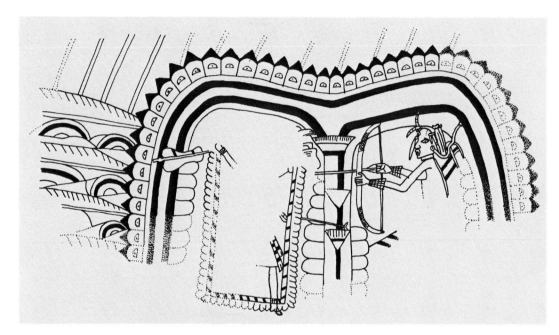

XXIV a). Possible Mississippian torture or sacrifice.

XXIV b). Natchez Indians torturing a war captive, early eighteenth century.

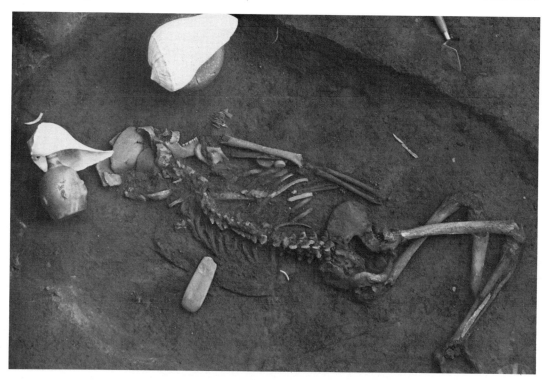

XXV a). Mississippian high status burial, Tennessee.

XXV b). Mortuary ceremony of the Natchez war leader.

Plate XXVI

Late Prehistory

XXVI a). Mississippian chunkey stone, Georgia.

XXVI b). Chunkey player, Mississippian shell gorget.

XXVI c). Mandan Indians playing chunkey.

XXVII a). Peregrine falcon.

XXVII b). Falcon dancer, Etowah.

Plate XXVIII

Late Prehistory

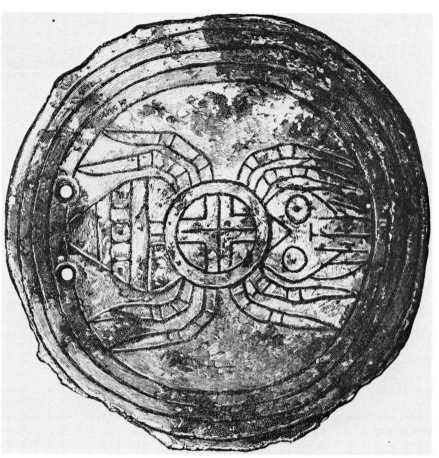

XXIX b). Wild turkeys on a shell cup from Spiro.

XXIX a). Wild turkey.

Plate XXX   *Late Prehistory*

XXX a). Ivory-billed woodpecker.

XXX b). Mississippian woodpecker gorget.

XXXI b). Anomalous cougar, shell cup from Spiro.

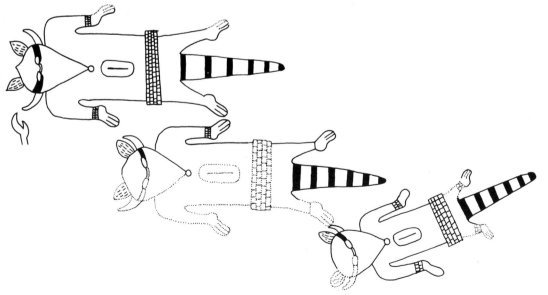

XXXI a). Raccoons on a shell cup from Spiro.

Plate XXXII   *Late Prehistory*

XXXII a). Diamondback rattlesnake.

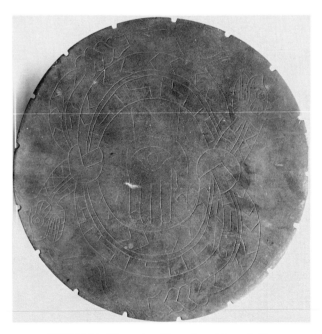

XXXII b). Horned rattlesnakes, Moundville.

XXXIII a). Winged horned serpent, Mound-ville.

XXXIII c). Fantastic fish-deer, shell cup from Spiro.

XXXIII b). Anomalous rattlesnake gorget, Tennessee.

Plate XXXIV *Late Prehistory*

XXXIV a). Men performing a ritual, Mississippian period.

XXXIV b). Men performing a ritual, Mississippian period.

XXXV b). Page from a Cherokee medicine man's book of sacred formulas.

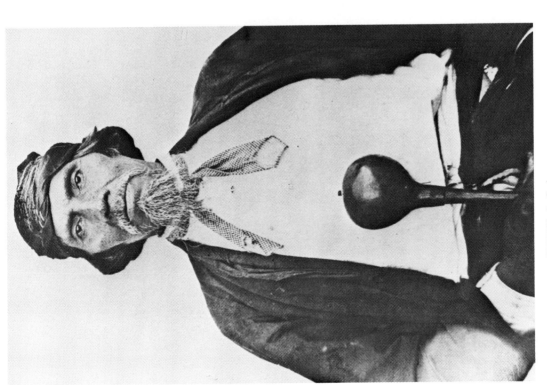

XXXV a). Swimmer.

Plate XXXVI   *Cherokee Cosmos*

XXXVI. Stone statues, Etowah.

XXXVII a). Fish pot, Mississippian period.

XXXVII b). Dog bottle, Mississippian period.

XXXVII c). Tomochichi and Tooanahowi with bald eagle.

Plate XXXVIII

Cherokee Cosmos

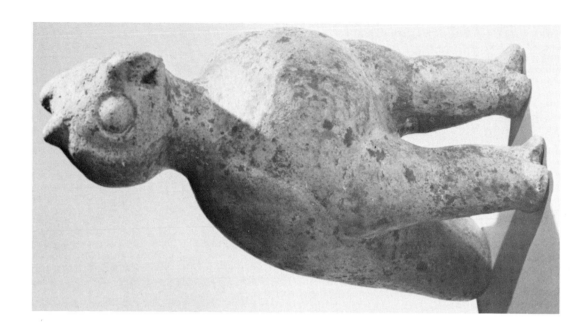

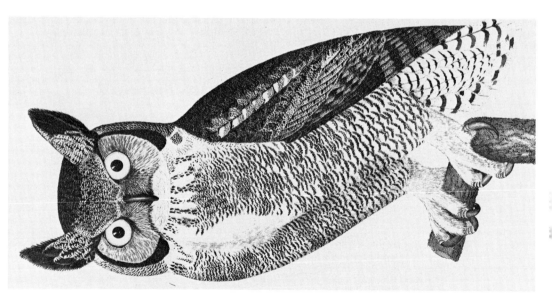

XXXIX b). Belted kingfisher.

XXXIX a). Bear pot, Mississippian period.

XXXIX c). Probable belted kingfisher, Mississippian
shell gorget.

Plate XL   *Cherokee Curing*

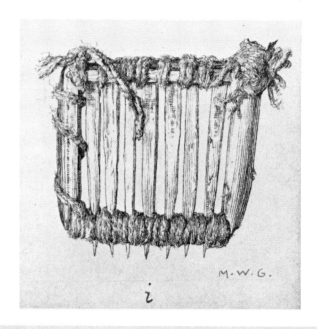

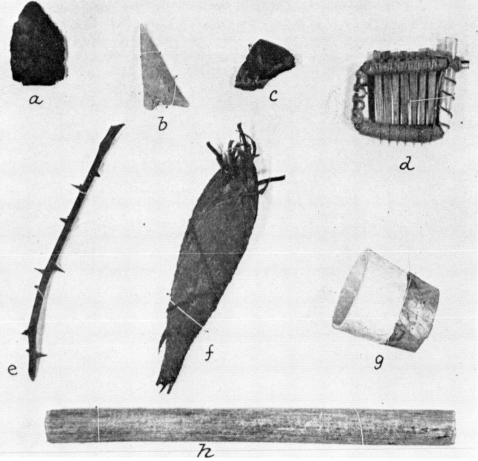

XL. Cherokee surgical instruments.

XLI b). Cherokee medicine man collecting a medicinal root.

XLI a). Cherokee medicine man scratching a stickball player.

Plate XLII

Cherokee Divination

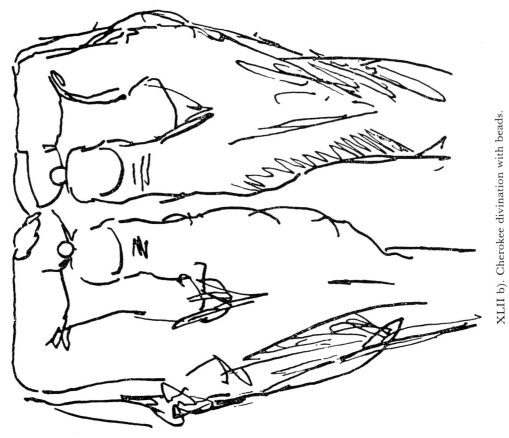

XLII b). Cherokee divination with beads.

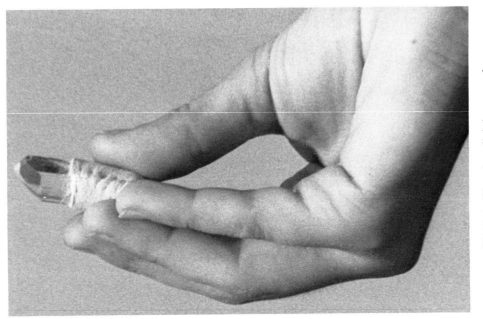

XLII a). Cherokee divining crystal.

XLIII. Creek green corn ceremony.

Plate XLIV   *Green Corn Ceremony*

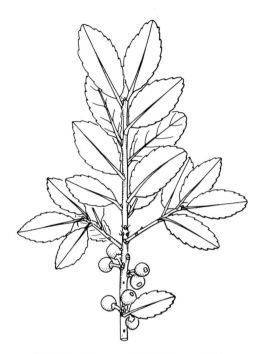

XLIV a). Yaupon holly (*Ilex vomitoria*).

XLIV b). Timucuan Indians drinking black drink.

XLV a). Devils carrying away an Indian.

XLV b). San Juan de Aspalaga, a Spanish mission in Florida.

Plate XLVI

Missionaries and Prophets

XLVI a). Samuel A. Worcester mission house, New Echota, Georgia.

XLVI b). Reconstructed printing shop at New Echota, Georgia.

XLVII. Redbird Smith and associates.

Plate XLVIII   *Missionaries and Prophets*

XLVIII a). Cherokee stickball dance.

XLVIII b). Cherokee stickball game.